COYOTE RECON

The Forgotten Wars of Colonel Jay D. Vanderpool

MIKE GUARDIA

Copyright 2022 © Mike Guardia

Published by Magnum Books
PO Box 1661
Maple Grove, MN 55311

www.mikeguardia.com

ISBN-13: 979-8-9854285-9-9

All rights reserved, including the right to reproduce this book or any part of this book in any form by any means including digitized forms that can be encoded, stored, and retrieved from any media including computer disks, CD-ROM, computer databases, and network servers without permission of the publisher except for quotes and small passages included in book reviews. Copies of this book may be purchased for educational, business or promotional use. Contact the publisher for pricing.

For Mom, Dad, Marie and Melanie,

and

To the memory of
Melba Caldera Guardia
(1934–2022)

Also by Mike Guardia

The Combat Diaries
Hal Moore: A Soldier Once . . . and Always
Skybreak
Days of Fury
Danger Forward
American Guerrilla
Shadow Commander

Co-authored with LTG Harold G. Moore

Hal Moore on Leadership:
Winning When Outgunned and Outmanned

CONTENTS

Introduction 1
CHAPTER 1 Dust Bowl Refugee 5
CHAPTER 2 Dawn Like Thunder 17
CHAPTER 3 Blood Red Shores 39
CHAPTER 4 Behind Enemy Lines 55
CHAPTER 5 After the Fire 117
CHAPTER 6 This Kind of War 131
CHAPTER 7 Winged Sabers 149
CHAPTER 8 The Winter Soldier 177
Epilogue 203
Select Bibliography 207
Notes 209
About the Author 213

Introduction

December 7, 1941: Second Lieutenant Jay D. Vanderpool, a Field Artillery officer stationed at Schofield Barracks, Hawaii, awakens to the sights and sounds of the Japanese attack on Pearl Harbor. By the end of the day, he is among the handful of survivors digging trenches and emplacing howitzers along the beaches of Oahu, anticipating a Japanese invasion of the Hawaiian Islands. But this dastardly attack on Pearl Harbor wasn't the first time Vanderpool had been in a high-stakes situation . . . nor would it be his last.

Jay Dee Vanderpool joined the Army as an enlisted man in 1936. A native of Oklahoma, he was orphaned by the age of 16, and joined the military as a means to escape the Dust Bowl and the ongoing Great Depression. Assigned to the Hawaiian Department as an artilleryman, he achieved the rank of Staff Sergeant by 1940. Despite being a high school dropout, he was accepted into Officer Candidate Training and became a Field Artillery officer in April 1941.

Following the attack on Pearl Harbor, he deployed to the Pacific with the 25th Infantry Division, where he fought in the Battles of Guadalcanal and New Georgia before volunteering for a highly-classified "liaison" mission to the Allied guerrillas in the Philippines. Infiltrating the Philippine Islands by submarine, Jay Vanderpool made contact with the Allied guerrillas in southern Luzon, and coordinated their operations with the 11th Airborne Division, facilitating the raid on the infamous Los Baños Prison Camp.

After the war, Vanderpool remained on active duty. Capitalizing on the unconventional warfare tactics he had learned in the Pacific, Jay subsequently commanded the United Nations Partisan Forces Korea (UNPFK) during the Korean War. These indigenous UN partisans (whose ranks included North Korean and Chinese defectors) conducted raids, tactical sabotage, and reconnaissance operations against high-value Communist targets.

Throughout the 1950s, Vanderpool became a leading advocate for helicopter warfare. He envisioned using the helicopter as both a close air support weapon *and* as a mobile troop carrier—delivering troops to the battlefield in a manner similar to the airborne infantry. At the rank of Lieutenant Colonel, he became one of the few senior officers in the Army to receive flight training and a subsequent rating as a helicopter pilot. In this regard, he became one of the "founding fathers" of airmobile (air assault) warfare.

Following his retirement at the rank of Colonel in 1967, Jay Vanderpool settled in Sarasota, Florida. But even in retirement, Vanderpool's legacy endured as a plank holder of helicopter warfare. In 1977, he was inducted into the Army Aviation Association of America's Hall of Fame, wherein he was cited as an unequivocal progenitor of the modern attack helicopter. Jay Vanderpool and his wife, Adelyn, remained in Sarasota, Florida until his death on June 16, 1993.

I am indebted to several individuals who have helped make this project a reality. Special thanks are reserved for Mr. Paul Bless, who first suggested that I undertake a biography of Jay D. Vanderpool. I had previously encountered Vanderpool's name in 2008 when

Introduction

I was conducting research for my first book, *American Guerrilla*. During the course of that research, I discovered that Jay Vanderpool was one among several Americans who were coordinating Allied guerrilla operations in the Philippines during World War II. I came across Vanderpool's name again in 2011 when compiling data for *Hal Moore: A Soldier Once . . . and Always*. Therein, I discovered that Vanderpool had played a critical role in the development of airmobile warfare. However, acting upon Mr. Bless's recommendation, I was amazed to discover the depth of Vanderpool's military service and the incredible backstory that shaped his approach to military life.

I am also indebted to the courteous, attentive, and hard-working staff at the US Army's Military History Institute in Carlisle Barracks, Pennsylvania. When I made the decision to pursue this biography, I knew that there would be limited resources available. Indeed, by the fall of 2021, Jay Vanderpool had been deceased for nearly thirty years. His widow, Adelyn, passed away in 2001. Their marriage produced no children. Jay's last surviving brother passed away in 2007. Tragically, one of Vanderpool's only surviving relatives with extensive knowledge of him, the Seattle-based columnist Myra Vanderpool Gormley, passed away in June 2020. With few immediate resources, MHI provided me with a wealth of information from his collection of personal papers on-file. Dubbed the "Jay D. Vanderpool Collection," this series includes various pieces of correspondence, photographs, and the transcript from an oral history interview given to the Army War College in 1983. Without the collective help of these individuals, this book may never have been written.

In a career that spanned more than thirty years, Jay D. Vanderpool proved himself to be a tough, resilient, and visionary leader.

His legacy endures today as a plank holder of American special operations and a "founding father" of modern helicopter warfare. Like the proverbial "coyotes" who stealthily run people across international borders, Jay Vanderpool earned his legacy by running Allied commandos behind enemy lines in North Korea and the Pacific.

Coyote Recon is his story.

1

Dust Bowl Refugee

The story of Jay Dee Vanderpool begins on the dusty plains of the American Southwest. Born on April 22, 1917 in Wetumka, Oklahoma, he was the eldest of four sons born to Dixon O. Vanderpool, an itinerant construction worker, and Edna "Bessie" Vanderpool (neé Smith). By all accounts, the Vanderpools were made of true pioneer stock. "One side of my family was English, Dutch, and Flemish," he said. "The other [half] was variously traced through the Indian territories and the frontier elements."

Growing up on the former frontier, Jay's upbringing reflected the rough-and-tumble lifestyle of his pioneering forebearers. "Most of my life was spent travelling somewhere," he said. "My father was in construction work and he had to go wherever there was something to build, so he could make a living." Thus, every few years, the Vanderpools would move to follow the tides of Dixon's commercial building projects. Indeed, by the time Jay was 16, he had lived in Oklahoma, New Mexico, Arizona, and California. "I guess that's one reason the Army routine didn't bother me," he reflected, "because I had been accustomed to doing that all my life anyway."

Yet, in every new town and at every new school, Jay immersed himself in the local variety of team sports—particularly football. "I wasn't very good at it," he admitted, "but I enjoyed the game."

Still, his enthusiasm was enough to land him a place on the varsity team.

His itinerant lifestyle, however, meant that he would play under several different coaches. "I had one year of high school in Deming, New Mexico;" he recalled, "two years of high school in Yuma, Arizona; and one year of high school in Wetumka, Oklahoma."

As the eldest boy in the family, Jay was expected to help care for his three younger brothers—Hoyt, Ray, and Norman. "They, of course, lived the same lifestyle I did as a youngster," said Jay—a life of transience, hard labor, and a thrifty pioneer work ethic. Not surprisingly, all four brothers eventually served in the Armed Forces. "All of us were in the military during World War II," he continued, "in one service or another." Norman and Hoyt both served in the Navy, whereupon Hoyt chose the path of a career sailor. "He retired as a chief petty officer," said Jay. "My third brother [Ray] was in the Army Signal Corps."

Although Dixon Vanderpool's construction work had been plentiful during the 1920s, the family's collective fortunes changed in the wake of the Great Depression. Indeed, the economic turmoil of the 1930s had robbed the family of their primary source of income. To make matters worse, Dixon and Bessie's marriage began to break down. When they married in July 1916, Dixon was 38, but Bessie was only 19. Dixon had been married twice before, and had fathered a son who tragically passed away as an infant in 1908. Although his union with Bessie lasted longer than his previous marriages, the couple divorced and Jay never saw his father again. Sadder still, Bessie passed away in February 1934, two months shy of Jay's seventeenth birthday.

"I was living with my mother when she died," he said. "She and my father were divorced, and I hadn't seen my father for several years." Straddled by the emotional burden of having an estranged father *and* a deceased mother, the young Jay Vanderpool and his three siblings were on their own. Bessie's untimely death meant that Jay had to quit school . . . and find a job in the middle of the Great Depression. "My mother died during my last year of school, so I went to work and didn't get my diploma."

As if the job market wasn't bad enough, Jay also had to contend with Mother Nature. Indeed, Oklahoma had become Ground Zero in the now-infamous "Dust Bowl." Decades of poor farming practices had damaged the topsoil in the high plains of Oklahoma, Kansas, Colorado, and Texas. With the onset of a severe drought, and the region's perennially high winds, the parched and brittle soil gave rise to massive dust storms. Many of these storms lasted for days, with winds approaching hurricane-force velocities. The prevailing winds often created dust clouds so thick that they literally blacked out the sun. Nicknamed "black blizzards" or "black rollers," they often reduced visibility to less than three feet (one meter) in any direction, and caused no end of respiratory problems for those who inhale the airborne dust.

But for Jay Vanderpool, the bigger problem was simply finding a job. To that end, he found a lifeline, of sorts, in the work programs of the New Deal. "I went to the CCC Camp"—the Civilian Conservation Corps—"which was something to do during the Depression years for kids that age without a good job." Indeed, the CCC put hundreds of thousands of young men to work—building roads, bridges, check dams, irrigation systems, even parks and picnic grounds. "I spent a little over a year with them," he said. "It was mostly hard physical work, which didn't bother me, because I had been raised on ranches and farms all my life. I was accustomed to hard work."

It was just as well; because his duties in the CCC gave him a 50-hour work week.

"I was able to carry on my natural liking for the mountains and timber country, the wild animals, and just being away from the cities," he continued. "I'd been raised out in New Mexico and Arizona. One time in New Mexico, our nearest neighbor was 16 miles away. I grew up in the environment of the range, the mountains, hunting and trapping."

Reflecting on his time in the CCC, Vanderpool said the discipline he learned in the camp helped him immensely when he joined the Army. In fact, many of the CCC camps were run by active duty Army officers—"and they did a fine job," he said. The camp culture was even structured along military lines—"the reveilles, the making up of beds . . . being punctual. When told to do something, you did it. You didn't debate it. It was very similar to being an enlisted man."

After a year in the CCC, Jay Vanderpool decided to leave the confines of the New Deal work program.

He packed what little he owned and headed west.

Now as a stereotypical "Dust Bowl Refugee," he joined the ever-growing ranks of displaced "Okies" as they migrated west in search of better work and higher wages. By most accounts, California was said to be the "promised land"—with perennial springtime weather and plenty of jobs in Depression-proof industries. The reality, however, was that the economy in California wasn't much better than it was throughout the rest of the country.

Still, the young teenaged Vanderpool was never hard up for employment. "I worked on what is now the All-American Canal, which paid a huge salary in those days. I drew 80 cents an hour driving a truck.[1] Then, after putting in an eight-hour shift driving a truck, I took another four-hour shift as a day laborer, which gave me a twelve-hour working day. I made a lot more money that way."

And he stayed with various kinfolk as he migrated westward.

"I'd stay with a relative and work nearby, then go visit some other relatives, stay a few months, and contribute to the household expenses there. At the time, they were all happy to have another wage earner in the household. I was *always* a wage earner. For one thing, I was flexible. A married man with a family can't get up and move overnight. But a teenage kid can, if he has some place to stay until he can make a little money." If Jay didn't like a particular area, or if his job prospects suddenly evaporated, he simply went elsewhere and found another job. "I kept just enough money to take care of myself for a few weeks until I got my first paycheck."

Meanwhile, the Vanderpool brothers scattered to the four winds. Each brother tried to find his own path while navigating life as a functional orphan. Still, the brothers remained in close contact for the rest of their lives. Years later, they learned that their estranged father, Dixon, had passed away in September 1941 at the age of 63.

Jay's travels ultimately landed him in Los Angeles. But, admittedly, he wasn't fond of Tinseltown or its residents. "I didn't like the environment," he said, "and there weren't any good jobs." Despite the allure and mystique of the California lifestyle, the Great Depression had nevertheless taken its toll on the Golden State.

"So, in December 1936, I enlisted in the Army," he said.

"I had no idea of being a career soldier, but I figured it was a good chance to travel around the country, get room and board, and see a lot." Little did he know that this "enlistment" would precipitate a 30-year career and a distinguished combat record in three of America's greatest conflicts.

Initially, however, Jay wanted to be a Marine. He walked into the Marine Corps recruiting station, and was initially accepted for service . . . until the Marines determined that he was "too short." Standing at 5 feet, 8 inches (nearly the average height for a man in 1936), Jay was astounded how the Marines could consider him "too short" for duty. He had passed the initial height screening only because he had been wearing cowboy boots, which added an extra inch-and-a-half to his frame. "So, they tore up my papers and sent me down the street to the Army recruiting station."

As it turned out, the Army had some choice assignments available in Panama and Hawaii. Jay took a particular interest, however, in the Pack Artillery units stationed along the Panama Canal. As their name implied, Pack Artillery was a highly-mobile, lightweight artillery system deployed by pack animals—in this case, mules.

But here again, Jay's height became a problem.

"You had to be 5-foot-10 for the Pack Artillery in Panama," he said. "You had to be taller to pick up those heavy artillery loads and put them on a mule." The recruiter then offered him another choice:

"Where do you want to go—the Philippines or Hawaii?"

"Hawaii," Jay replied.

Both locations had their appeal. And Jay figured that he could begin his service in Hawaii, then transfer to the Philippines at a later date.

Within a few weeks of swearing his oath, 19-year-old Jay Vanderpool arrived at Schofield Barracks, Hawaii for Basic Training as an artilleryman. Basic Training in the 1930s, however, bore little resemblance to its modern-day counterpart. "They took the replacements and put us all into a pool of infantry and artillery. I think we had some Engineer people in there too," he said. "So, we all had about four months of Basic Training in Schofield under the supervision of officers and noncommissioned officers."

The young Vanderpool took readily to the Army lifestyle. Indeed, his rough and rural upbringing had prepared him well. Aside from his father's construction work, Jay recalled that: "We used to go broke raising cows. Everyone raised cattle. We also raised a lot of alfalfa hay. Well, hay hauling is hard work." Taken together, his frontiersman upbringing and impeccable work ethic were enough to earn Jay the award for "top recruit" of his training cycle. In later years, he admitted that he was prouder of his Basic Training "hero badge" than any other award he received in the military.

Reflecting on his daily instruction as a new recruit, "the mornings were common subjects," he said, "then in the afternoon from one o' clock to four, we went into our unit training—our specialized infantry, engineer, or artillery; whatever it might be. We had a common basic training and a special individual training by your arm of service."

Upon graduation, Vanderpool was assigned to the 8th Field Artillery Regiment.

"We supported the 22d Infantry Brigade, which then consisted of the 27th and 35th Infantry Regiments." These units (including Jay's regiment), belonged to the US Army's "Hawaiian Division." Unlike the numbered divisions, the Army kept a handful of *named* divisions based upon their territorial location. For instance, there was a Philippine Division, Panama Canal Division, and Americal Division (New Caledonia). The Hawaiian Division was eventually disbanded, with its units parceled out to the newly-activated 24th and 25th Infantry Divisions.

This was, however, the lithe and lean Army of the prewar years. Congress, in the midst of its isolationist fervor, kept the War

Department on little more than a shoestring budget. As a result, the Hawaiian and Philippine contingents perennially subsisted on less than half of what they needed to perform their regular missions. "I had volunteered for artillery," said Jay, "but I think I was there [at my unit] about six months before I ever got near a gun." Indeed, Private Vanderpool had been assigned to the Regimental Headquarters Battery as a *radio operator*.

"I tried to get transferred to a lettered battery so I could get gun drill."

After all, he didn't want his core competencies as an artilleryman to atrophy while he sat behind a communications console. His battery leadership, however, was less than enthusiastic.

"Oh, you don't need that," they told him.

"We'll let you go out to gun drill sometime."

But as the months passed, Jay realized he'd have to take matters into his own hands. "I did that on my own in the afternoons"—going down to the line batteries and sitting in on their cannon crew drills.

"In my regiment, we had the British 75"—a WWI-era field gun capable of firing the standard 75mm QF rounds. Of course, the lack of funding meant that there were very little "live fire" drills for the howitzer batteries. Most of these gun drills were, in effect, dry runs. Still, the young Vanderpool enjoyed whatever crew training he could get. "Until World War II started," he recalled, "I did all my training on the British 75."

Still, he could not escape his daily duties as a radioman. "I went to radio school for four or five months," which taught him the dubious skill of writing nearly two dozen radio code groups per minute.

"I was never able to write legibly again," he joked.

But even as a radioman, he participated in maneuvers all over the island of Oahu. It was during these select maneuvers that the cannon crews received their best live fire training. "We had, in Hawaii," he said, "a large supply of conventional ammunition—the 75mm. Well, after Dunkirk [1940], the British were really short on ammunition.[2] We drew down to a few days' fire and shipped the rest of it off to Britain."

Jay sympathized with the British and their plight; but this massive consignment of ammunition left the American batteries on Oahu dangerously low on firepower. For if the Hawaiian contingent had to fight off a Japanese land invasion, the Americans would burn through that "few days' fire" in a matter of hours. But, as Jay conceded, "that was an economic thing that was not going to be resolved in the atmosphere that our country was in during the Depression."

By the fall of 1940, however, the political climate was much different than it had been when Jay joined the Army in 1936. Isolationism still rang high in the halls of Congress, but that ideology was quickly losing steam as Nazi Germany advanced on all fronts. Determined to stem the tide of Nazi aggression, even if by passive means, Congress passed the Lend-Lease Act in 1941. Under the terms of Lend-Lease, the US sent several pieces of military equipment to Great Britain and the Soviet Union in their ongoing struggle against the *Wehrmacht*.

Almost simultaneously, the US government authorized a full-scale increase in military spending. Still, many Americans hoped that the war in Europe would run its course without their involvement.

The Empire of Japan, however, was of little concern to anyone at this point.

Despite their recent aggressions on mainland China, most were certain that the Japanese could *never* challenge the US military.

But as the situation in Europe and the Pacific went from bad to worse, Jay Vanderpool enjoyed the downstream effects of the newfound defense money. "We intensified our field training," he said. "When we got enough gasoline [a scarce commodity in the Depression-era Army] we were able to hold some maneuvers, and we had some pretty good maneuvers. Our headquarters was at Pearl City, because we were working in defense of southern Oahu from Ewa over on the west to Diamond Head on the east. We got in some good command post exercises, and I think that the regimental and brigade staff officers got more experience that year in 1941 than they'd had in years because we finally had enough gasoline and money."

These maneuvers also facilitated a better synchronicity between the infantry and artillery units. "Infantry and artillery commanders didn't speak to one another except under duress in those days," Jay recalled; "those old colonels wouldn't talk to one another." Organizational rivalries aside, these maneuvers also exposed shortcomings in the Army's tactical communications. As a reluctant radioman, Jay Vanderpool had a front row seat to the liabilities of the Army's field networks.

"The biggest problem was our weakness in our radio system," he said.

"We had an excellent hand-laid wire system, if trucks or somebody didn't tear it up. But the radios were just too weak for the missions we were assigned." Indeed, these were World War I-era radio sets, with shorter broadcasting ranges—"for massed troops in Europe," he added. "They were not adequate to cover *our* area. We even devised our own systems of top loading antennas and things like that to try to enhance the range. Communication was probably our single biggest problem; but we had good wire, supplemented by limited radio and motorcycle couriers."

In the spring of 1941, having distinguished himself as a young staff sergeant, Jay Vanderpool was selected to attend Officer Candidate Training. Prior to the official establishment of the Army's Officer Candidate School, pre-war selectees attended a "home study course," as Jay called it, supplemented by classroom instruction at the local garrison. "The basic course was a ten series," he said—conducted in-house at the Oahu facilities.

"In our artillery brigade," he continued, "we had a school of volunteers whose regimental commanders thought they were officer material. We could go to school two hours a day and an optional two hours more at night. I went in the afternoon. I used to teach at night because a lot of people were rusty on some subjects such as trigonometry [a critical skill for artillery calculations]. We taught communications, tactics, and survey among other subjects. From those studies, we took a little written examination. It lasted about half a day or so."

Then came the field examination.

During this practical exam, the officer candidate assumed the role of a battery commander—"commanding a battery, giving all the orders, putting the battery into position, and firing with live ammunition, which is as good a training as you can give to a sergeant," said Vanderpool. "So, I thought they had a pretty good program. I got my second lieutenant bars in the spring of 1941. That's the reason I was a second lieutenant when the war started."

Coincidentally, one of Jay's earliest comrades during this time was a young William Westmoreland—who served alongside him in the 8th Field Artillery Regiment. "I think he was a first lieutenant when I was a sergeant, and a captain when I was a second lieutenant." A 1936 West Point graduate, Westmoreland would rise to fame (and subsequent notoriety) as the commander of American forces in Vietnam. But, during his days as a young company-grade officer in Hawaii, Vanderpool remembered Westmoreland as: "sort of quiet, hardworking, and very, very serious." Jay continued: "When he went to work, he was all work and no play. But off duty, he was relaxed. He went to athletic games and boxing matches. He was always trying to support the regimental sports, and I know he coached basketball. At the time, regimental sports were a big thing." In fact, every soldier in the regiment was encouraged to participate in at least two seasonal sports per year.

As a newly-minted second lieutenant, Jay Vanderpool was assigned to the Regimental Operations Staff (S-3), responsible for drafting and implementing the regiment's training schedule. Having worked in the Headquarters Battery, he already had a good familiarity with the work flow of the various staff sections.

But as Jay settled into his new role as a commissioned officer, Japan's war of aggression was about to make landfall in Hawaii.

2

Dawn Like Thunder

By the fall of 1941, the US War Department knew that hostilities were imminent. It was not a question of *if*... but *when*. "We all knew the war was coming," said Vanderpool. "We just didn't know the exact date." Surprisingly, however, Jay admitted that his chain-of-command knew an *approximate* date for when the war would start.

"We were estimating January 1st," he said, "plus or minus 30 days."

Sometime before the attack on Pearl Harbor, Jay Vanderpool and his fellow officers were called into the briefing theater at Fort Shafter.

"We all went in, and closed and locked the doors," he recalled. "The commanding general [Walter Short] came in and told us he had just returned from Washington, where he'd just talked to the President. We were to be told, but not to repeat it outside of that room (until the war was over), that we were going to war with Japan, about the first of January, plus or minus a month or so." The general likewise told his officers to memorize their battle positions—"so we could get there in a hurry," Jay added.

By now, the latter-day Hawaiian Division had been dissolved; and the 8th Artillery Regiment had been reassigned to the newly-created 25th Infantry Division.[3] This reorganization, however, had done nothing to alleviate the territorial readiness issues. For even if the Hawaiian units could occupy their battle positions "in a hurry," they didn't have enough ammunition to hold off the Japanese for long. "We were also told during the briefing that the United States would not publicly attack the Emperor of Japan, but his governmental officials. The reason being was that we would need the Emperor of Japan after the war to control the nation."

Surprisingly, Jay and his comrades were unalarmed by the general's remarks.

"There was no surprise except the date," he said, "because every officer in that theater *knew* it was coming, and I haven't seen that [briefing] repeated in writing anywhere; but I know I was there in the theater . . . I believe it was General Short who gave us that briefing."[4]

Jay had no idea how the War Department (or any other government office) had determined their "January 1st" ETA. But for now, the bigger question was: *Where would the Japanese strike first?*

Hawaii?

The Philippines?

San Francisco?

He didn't know.

Nevertheless, he would occupy his battle position whenever the time came.

As it turned out, Jay Vanderpool wouldn't have to wait for long.

"We had a perimeter defense mission," he said. "The main idea was to meet them [the enemy] on beaches to take them under fire at the beach, and then use the reserves . . . for counterattacks or containing penetrations." Although the perimeter defense had put the regiment's maximum firepower forward, Jay noted that their assigned beachfronts lacked a sufficient amount of "tactical depth."

All told, the 8th Artillery Regiment would be little more than a speedbump against a Japanese landing force.

On the morning of December 7, 1941, Jay Vanderpool awoke to the sights and sounds of the attack on Pearl Harbor. The first wave of enemy planes arrived shortly before 8:00 AM, targeting Battleship Row and the nearby facilities at Hickam and Wheeler Army Air Fields. "At Schofield," he said, "they strafed anything that moved." Indeed, whenever a brave soldier jumped into a vehicle, or tried to assemble a convoy, the marauding Japanese Zeroes would cut him down in a hail of gunfire—"they were trying to prevent any movement or reinforcement." Thus, while Hickam Field and Battleship Row went up in flames, the 8th Artillery Regiment was helplessly pinned down.

"We didn't get into our field positions until about sundown that night," he admitted.

"In our battalion, I think we had two killed . . . five or six wounded. At Wheeler Field, down the road about three or four miles, they really got chewed up because they had their planes lined up and the Japs came along and strafed them."

Battleship Row, however, had borne the brunt of the Japanese assault. Indeed, all eight of the *Pennsylvania*-class battleships at Pearl Harbor had sustained critical damage, with the *Arizona* and *Oklahoma* being totally destroyed. The Imperial Japanese Navy had hoped to crush the Pacific Fleet in one blow, thus crippling America's ability to wage war in the Pacific. Ironically, the Japanese may have succeeded if the US aircraft carriers had not been away from Pearl Harbor on maneuver.

Throughout the morning of December 7th, outlandish rumors spread almost as quickly as the enemy gunfire. Several times throughout the day, Vanderpool and his comrades heard that Oahu was under siege from a fleet of Japanese invasion ships. "Well," said Vanderpool, "according to rumors, [the Japanese ships] were coming in about every 30 minutes from different directions. We sent a man to Kolekole Pass to see if he could spot anything coming. The Japs were strafing the fishing boats west of Oahu that morning. So, all the fishermen decided the best thing to do was get over on the beach, and get away from the Japanese fire . . . 40–50 fishing boats heading to the beach." Meanwhile, the young officer atop Kolekole Pass (perhaps in a state of panic-induced delirium) reported these incoming fishing boats as a Japanese landing force. "He didn't report what he *saw*; he reported what he *deduced*," Jay said with a chuckle. "He saw boats coming to the beach, and to him that was the landing force."

But the fact remained that American blood had been spilled on American soil.

The US was now at war with the Empire of Japan.

"We got out to our assigned area [along the beach] and started digging in," said Jay—scanning the horizon for any sign of Japanese landing craft. For their deployment to the beach, Jay's unit received a battery of so-called "beach guns"—mobile, direct-fire artillery pieces adapted for shoreline defenses. "We had positions dug along the east coast line (Kailua-Waimanalo), with 'Panama' concrete circular mounts," he said. "We dropped the guns on those. They were covered and camouflaged with sand. I had 12 of those guns that I dropped in that night."

Incidentally, one of these gun positions occupied the front yard of a lady named Mrs. Fleming. As Jay recalled, Fleming was a middle-aged woman whose husband and children were actively serving. "Her two daughters were in the Red Cross," he said, "she had two sons in the Navy on PT boats over at Kaneohe; and her husband was off somewhere in the mountains [for emergency muster] in some kind of reserve unit."

But when Jay came upon Mrs. Fleming's front yard, she was furiously digging her own foxhole. "She had a foxhole about five feet deep and three feet long," he marveled. "She was just sweating and throwing dirt all over the place. She had a big old double-barrel shot gun and several boxes of buckshot."

"Ma'am, what are you doing?" he asked.

"I'm going to kill those bastards," she snarled. "If they come across this beach, I'm going to kill them!"

Jay was both impressed and amused.

"That was our first line of ground defense out there," he said. Indeed, Vanderpool's artillerymen (and the stalwart Mrs. Fleming) were the farthest rung of Allied defenders on Oahu that night.

The following day, the US declared war on the Empire of Japan. With the stroke of a pen, America had officially entered World War II. Germany soon responded, however, by declaring war on the United States, thus forcing the US into a two-front conflict.

Although Japan had initiated hostilities, the US adopted a "Europe First" policy—meaning that, while fighting on two fronts, Europe would be the priority. The reasoning behind this decision was that Germany could win the war without Japan, but Japan couldn't win the war without Germany. Nevertheless, the US prepared itself for war against the Rising Sun.

"One of the first things we did," said Vanderpool, "was get some American-made 105mm artillery to replace our British 75s." It was just as well, considering that the American batteries had already forfeited most of their ammunition back to the British via the Lend-Lease Act. "We got the new guns," Vanderpool continued, "and we got a lot of new communications gear that we had been needing for years, but didn't have the money. We got new fire direction equipment; all brand new. We finally had a high priority back in the War Department to ship all the latest stuff out to us." Alongside the new 105mm howitzers, Jay remembered that the medium-weight artillery battalions received the new Split Trail 155mm gun—"which gave them better mobility and a faster firing rate, too."

Around this time, the 25th Infantry Division also received an influx of new personnel. This included a virtual flood of new enlistees . . . and a new division commander—Brigadier General J. Lawton Collins. A 1917 West Point graduate, he had been the Chief of Staff in the Hawaiian Department; and now at the age of 46, he was the youngest division commander in the Army. Vanderpool recalled that: "after the Solomon Campaigns, he went to Europe to command a corps [VII Corps], and was later Chief of Staff of the Army."

Vanderpool was also impressed by the number of Japanese-Americans who showed up to enlist. These included several of Hawaii's "Nisei" population—the "American-born Japanese kids," said Vanderpool. "I got 60 or 65 of them in one day," he said, "and they wanted to fight." These young Nisei men were infuriated by the actions of their ancestral homeland. "I'd have kept those kids all during the war if I'd been allowed to, but we weren't." Sadly, as Jay admitted: "They were pulled out, and sent back [to the US mainland] for training"—training that landed them in the segregated 442d Regimental Combat Team. Although a segregated unit, the 442d "Nisei" Regiment served with incredible distinction in the European Theater. In fact, more Medals of Honor came out of the

442d than any other unit in the war. To this day, the Nisei Regiment remains the most-decorated American unit of its size. "They were Cracker Jack kids," said Vanderpool.

Jay would also discover that the Army's new manpower needs would accelerate his promotion timelines. Indeed, that January, he received an unexpected promotion from second lieutenant to first lieutenant. Under peacetime conditions, Jay would not have been eligible for such a promotion until the spring of 1943, two years from his commissioning date. But now that the country was at war, the Army decreed that every officer who had at least six months time-in-grade would be promoted to the next higher rank. Jay Vanderpool thus received an early promotion to first lieutenant—"which you only do, of course, in wartime," he added.

By the summer of 1942, Jay Vanderpool had spent the past several months digging foxholes along the beaches of Oahu. However, when the War Department realized that an invasion of Hawaii was unlikely, American forces finally went on the offensive. "So, in the summer of 1942," said Jay, "we started loading convoys out for the south [Pacific]. Of course, you didn't tell soldiers where they were going. It would be all over town the next morning."

During these early days of the Pacific War, operational security was at its tightest.

This was, after all, the era of "Loose Lips Sink Ships."

Troop movements, rosters, and destinations were on a strict *need-to-know* basis.

"We started chugging off straight south," Jay continued—towards an unknown destination somewhere in the South Pacific. "We were aboard ship for, I don't know how many weeks, and those ships could only move at the speed of the slowest vessel in a convoy."

Still, the average speed of the troop carriers in Vanderpool's convoy was about eight knots—a steady pace, but not fast enough to outrun a Japanese sub.

In fact, as Vanderpool recalled: "We got a lot of submarine scares." Surprisingly, however, the enemy subs never scored a single hit. "I don't know how you could ever shoot that much and not hit someone!" he beamed. "I've seen three or four torpedoes in the water at one time. We were lucky, or their torpedoes were not much good."

Still, the convoy made it through submarine alley without losing a single ship.

For every nautical mile, however, the troop carriers were escorted by a fleet of destroyers. "Most of them were the old WWI four stackers," said Vanderpool. "They had the newer ones out on combat patrols. I think we had one heavy and one light cruiser. We'd see them every day or so; they'd come in and go out of sight. They didn't want to poke along at eight knots . . . also, they were running down reported sightings."

As it turned out, Vanderpool and the 25th Infantry Division were headed for Guadalcanal. It was America's first major offensive of the war, fought mostly by GIs with "too little experience and too little training."

Still, Guadalcanal would be the first step on the bloody road to Tokyo. Barring the exception at Midway, the Japanese had seen nothing but success throughout 1942. In May, however, a system of "Coastwatchers" (set up by the Australian Defence Force), reported to the Allies that the Japanese were building an airbase on Guadalcanal, a small island on the western edge of the Solomons. Such an airbase would put the Japanese within striking distance of the Australian sea lanes. Thus came the idea for Operation Watchtower, the plan to retake Guadalcanal and capture the enemy airbase. Due to the priority focus on Europe, however, the campaign for Guadalcanal became known as "Operation Shoestring."

The 1st Marine Division led the charge, landing on Guadalcanal in August 1942. Without any close air support, or naval gunfire, the battered Marines succeeded in capturing the airfield. By August 20, the first American planes touched down on Guadalcanal. The Japanese, meanwhile, fled into the jungle, determined to regroup and drive the Allies back into the sea.

In November 1942, the 2d Marine Division landed at Guadalcanal, followed soon by the 25th Infantry Division. The 2d Marine Division had arrived to relieve the battle-weary 1st Division troops on the line. By that time, the Americans had secured the airfield, and the new Army-Marine task force was preparing to drive the Japanese off the island. But the Americans' slapdash training, and their atrophied supply system, was now coming back to haunt them. As one Marine artilleryman recalled: "Our maps were so bad, we couldn't use them. I went up ahead to be a forward observer so we could hit what we were supposed to hit. Sometime later, I realized I was two or three hundred yards away from our troops."

To make matters worse, the humidity was stifling and it rained incessantly. But bad weather and supply issues notwithstanding, it often seemed that the local insects posed a greater threat than the Japanese. There were mosquitos, flies, leeches . . . and other creepy crawlers that most GIs had never heard of. In fact, during this time on Guadalcanal, more American troops died from malaria than from enemy fire.

But nothing could have prepared American GIs for the brutality (and borderline insanity) of a Japanese *banzai* attack. "The Japanese would get all sake'd up as the night went on," said one Marine. Saké was the enemy's drink of choice—an alcoholic beverage that, even when diluted, could lead to a quick state of inebriation. "Then they would charge en masse, yelling 'banzai,' and screaming like you've never heard before."

Still, the Marines had been standing strong in the face of enemy fire. "Someone decided to send us, the 25th Division, to reinforce and later replace the Marines," said Vanderpool. "The Marines were picking up pretty heavy casualties. The Second Marine Division was just getting bloodied when I got there."

En route to Guadalcanal, Jay received yet another unexpected promotion. "We had another policy that came down," he said, "that if you were in a job that called for a promotion, you got that promotion when you went up the gangplank." The GIs often called them "gang plank promotions." And because Jay was an S-3 staff officer, he was eligible for promotion to captain. "So, I made captain on the gangplank," he said. "I arrived in Guadalcanal as a captain."

Once within sight of the blood-stained island, Vanderpool's troop carrier pulled into the straits between Guadalcanal and Tulagi, turning northward to facilitate the GIs offloading onto their landing craft. Jay Vanderpool and his fellow cannoneers began their descent into the landing craft while the troop ship was still underway—travelling at "four, probably five knots when we went down the landing nets into the bouncing boats."

Jay's landing craft was the first to be released.

"The ship's officers were in a big hurry to get rid of us," he continued. "I'm sure they didn't want us hanging over the side on the net, where we might get shot any minute." However, the ship's crew had been so eager to dispatch the GIs, that they delivered them to the *wrong location*. "They released us five miles outside the

US perimeter," said Jay wryly. "We were in Jap territory which was so far behind the Japs, they didn't even notice us."

At first, Jay had no indication that he had been dropped behind enemy lines. But as his landing craft came ashore, he realized that something was amiss: "We did not notice any friendly US Marine activity. It was very quiet."

Indeed, a little *too* quiet.

"We looked around for tracks. We found some, but the tracks were made by soft-soled shoes. The big toe was separated from the other toes in the shoes"—the unmistakable imprint of Japanese footwear. It was then that Jay realized the troop carrier had delivered them to the wrong place.

Undaunted: "We set up a perimeter defense and sent out some outposts to watch and listen." One of the landing craft pilots, however, was well-verse in semaphore (naval flag) signaling, and had some flags aboard his vessel. "There were a number of US Navy combat ships and boats passing by," said Vanderpool. "The semaphore flags attracted attention at last. We were picked up and taken up the coast to our original destination . . . Lunga Point, Guadalcanal. That's out there on the peninsula . . . the beachhead near Henderson Field."

Still, that unwitting venture into Japanese territory had been an exciting way to start his combat tour. "We had a little beachhead of our own for about half a day," he joked. "We didn't fight anyone; there was no one to fight." Surprisingly, the enemy was nowhere to be found. "We scouted around," said Jay, "but they weren't there."

A few hours later, Jay Vanderpool arrived on the American beachhead near Lunga Point. He was with the so-called "advance party" of the 25th Infantry Division—the first wave of US Army personnel attached to the Marines on Guadalcanal. "I'm not sure what the organization for combat was, but we were told to report to the Marines for duty. We got down there and some personnel officer wanted to know what our specialties were; I told him mine [artillery]."

"Okay," said the officer. "You're assigned to the 11th Marine Regiment."

The 11th Regiment was an artillery unit supporting the 2nd Marine Division. As Jay recalled, the Marine Corps "numbered their regiments, indicating it was an artillery regiment supporting the infantry of that division."

As an attachment to the 11th Marines, Jay admired the tenacity and resilience of his seagoing comrades. "The leathernecks were there and they'd been fighting for a month or two. They'd had quite a bit of combat. They were using those little pack artillery guns, the 75mm." Ironically, these were the same guns from which Vanderpool had been barred to entry due to his alleged "height deficiency." Yet here he was, in 1942, serving in a pack artillery unit with no impediments caused by his 5'8" frame.

Although the Marines were fierce artillerymen, Vanderpool noted that the 75mm pack howitzers were "too light" for the magnitude of their fire missions. "It's kind of like shooting bird shot in the forest," he said. "It didn't do an awful lot of good; made lots of noise and sometimes you got a few casualties with them, but they were pretty light. I stayed with the Marines a few weeks until my division was ashore. I think my division was committed January 10; so sometime late in December or early January, I came back to my division. In the meantime, I was shooting cannon balls with Marine artillery over the National Guard infantry regiment's head."

Indeed, a handful of National Guard regiments had joined the fight for Guadalcanal. "The Marines had kindly given them Mount

Austen to take," said Vanderpool. "Mount Austen happened to be where just about all the remaining Japs in Guadalcanal were at that time. The Marines had estimated there was a reinforced platoon up there; but it was more than that, because when we got through, there were 3,000 dead on the battlefield."

And, as Jay recalled, the National Guard "really got its nose bloody."

In fact, one of their battalion commanders had been killed early during the battle.

"We were fighting hard," said Jay, "but the Japs were dug in—good solid bunkers logs and dirt with just little narrow firing slits. They were well-camouflaged; you usually wouldn't see them until within 20 or 30 feet. Usually, you heard them before you saw them." But by the time a soldier could *hear* them, he was already in the crossfire. "Therefore, when you hit them," Jay continued, "you lost quite a few men before you could even maneuver. When a platoon went up there, if they didn't lose the better part of one squad, they were lucky. It was real nasty, very close fighting up there on the mountain."

Jay also commented on the complexities of rendering fire support within a jungle environment. One of the biggest barriers was the jungle canopy itself. "Those trees looked to be 60 to 100 feet high," he said. "In order to get through the canopy of the dense rain forest, we had to use fuse delay"—an artillery projectile that would detonate on a time-delay instead of detonating on impact. Typically, an artillery officer had real-time access to naval gunfire.

Not so on Guadalcanal.

"They can't use it effectively where they can't see," he said wryly. For a close-quarters fight, "you don't want a big old 16-inch, or 12-inch, or 8-inch gun plopping in there and being off by 100 yards," he added. "You just can't pull Navy fire in real close like you can with field artillery fire, which has a high trajectory so it could drop almost straight down. The Navy fire is a very flat trajectory, so you have to fire it either on a rising slope or something level. I don't know of any case where it's effective as a close support weapon."

It was, however, highly effective as an area fire weapon.

"Area fire is where you don't worry if a few rounds go over—that's high velocity. If you're up just a few meters too high [with elevating the gun tube], you're going to go another mile [on the shell's trajectory]. Naval gunnery is good against targets they can see, but when firing into the woods, they just can't see the target."

Jay also realized that whenever the National Guard units sustained heavy casualties, it left a profound impact throughout their ranks. Very often, the members of a National Guard battalion or regiment had grown up alongside each other . . . in the same hometown. "They're all family, friends, and relatives," said Jay. Thus, seeing a lifelong friend killed in combat could have a devastating impact on a soldier's morale. As one officer recalled, these National Guard outfits "were essentially like hometown units, and they knew families; and it was a little more complicated than, say, a Regular Army unit where you may not know anybody's family when you have to send somebody up a hill."

As the Marines and National Guard continued their struggle for Mount Austen, the main body of the 25th Infantry Division came ashore.

"I went back with my own outfit," Jay said.

Now as part of the division's 161st Regimental Combat Team (RCT), Jay Vanderpool was assigned to the 89th Field Artillery Battalion. "We were shooting wherever they needed fire," he beamed. "We fought on Mount Austen for two or three more weeks. It was loaded with several thousand Japs up there . . . but my division finally took the objective, clearing the top of Mount Austen."

Casualties were high in the battle for Mount Austen; and it took several US regiments to subdue the enemy.

"Finally, we even got some light tanks up there," Jay added.

The Marines, of course, had been using their M2/M3 tank battalions since the early days of the campaign. In the 25th Infantry Division, however, tanks belonged to the division's reconnaissance troop. "And the best-qualified tanker we had," said Vanderpool, "was the commander of the reconnaissance troop. He usually drove the lead tank." Jay noted, however, that the tank's effectiveness could be hamstrung by unfavorable terrain—"these greasy, slimy, wet mountains," as he called them.

Still, Jay recalled that the Army and Marine Corps tanks were remarkably effective against enemy bunkers; and they had a profound *psychological* effect on the enemy. "Actual effectiveness, I think, was about 60 percent psychological . . . and about 40 percent normal fire effectiveness," he said. "They had to fight bunker by bunker. The Japs called the area the Gifu Strongpoint.[5] In the meantime, we were burning up everything that would burn, and trying to level everything that wouldn't burn with artillery and aerial bombs. The Japs were taking a terrific beating." But although the Americans had claimed the top of Mount Austen, there was a problem on the leeward side of the craggy peak.

"Right behind the mountain, there was a big canyon," said Jay.

Sprawled across this canyon floor was the enemy's logistics base and its tactical reserve area. But because this enemy base had occupied a *canyon*, it was beyond the reach of Allied naval gunfire.

"The Japs wouldn't get out of the canyon, and we didn't want to go down into it," Jay said. "We estimated there were between one and three thousand [enemy troops] down there. It's very dangerous going into a canyon full of mad Japs. So, we decided to sit on the hill and drop ammunition on them."

To that end, one of the naval gunfire liaisons offered a suggestion:

"I think we'll get some good echo effects down in that canyon; why not try it?"

Essentially, this liaison officer was recommending they drop airborne-delivered *depth charges* into the enemy canyon. Depth charges were anti-submarine weapons designed to destroy enemy vessels via shock wave. But as Jay Vanderpool admitted: "We were willing to try anything." Within minutes, the liaison officer had a flight of Navy planes overhead. "He dropped dozens and dozens of depth charges down into this canyon. Oh, they were noisy!"

But this explosive juggernaut soon yielded to dead silence.

When Vanderpool and his men descended into the canyon, they found that the Japanese reserve of 1,000+ men had been decimated to less than 200. "They were dead on the ground, blood running out of their ears, eyes popped out of their faces. A lot of them were just in shock. I've never seen such a horrible thing in my life as a bunch of people hit by high compression sound waves. It really knocked them out. We also found there was a hospital down there, reserve bivouac area for a couple of battalions, and everyone left was a casualty."

Securing the canyon, American forces crossed the Matanikau River, en route to a series of enemy-held ridges and two prominent hills codenamed "Sea Horse" and Galloping Horse." The objective, said Vanderpool, was to "try to take some ridges up there . . . which would help cut off reinforcements by sea or withdrawal of major formations."

Although the Japanese still held the advantage in terrain (they had dug their defensive lines onto the reverse slopes of the ridge network), the Americans succeeded in clearing the enemy from the hilltops. The attack on Galloping Horse Hill, led by the 27th Infantry Regiment, was halted twice by Japanese fire before the GIs overran the enemy defenses. During that melee, the regiment's 2d Battalion commander was killed in action. Undeterred, the battalion's young executive officer, Captain Charles Davis, rallied the survivors to an impressive victory that claimed the lives of no fewer than 170 enemy soldiers. For his actions that day, Davis was awarded the Congressional Medal of Honor.[6]

Reflecting on the campaign for Guadalcanal, Jay Vanderpool said: "I personally thought that our casualties were very, very light. Remember, we were killing 10 to 20 Japs for every one of our wounded. Of our wounded, three out of four lived. We were really making a tremendous offensive at what I thought then, and still do, was a fairly conservative cost. It's very bitter for a few minutes, or a few hours, or even a few days, but we were hitting them day and night. The Japs came in there with about 33–35,000 men [later confirmed to be more than 36,000]." By the end of the campaign, however, the Japanese had lost more than 20,000 men. "They evacuated what was left by submarine."

Jay was elated that the Americans had taken Guadalcanal. But he was also critical of his regiment's tactical pursuit operations during the latter days of the campaign. "At that time, the Japs were trying to disengage and pull off to our right flank to get out [of Guadalcanal]," he said. "Of course, we didn't know they were trying to evacuate; we knew they were trying to disengage, and we were trying to keep up with them and maintain contact. So, my regiment [the 161st RCT] was given the job of pursuit . . . to try to keep them from going wherever they might want to go." But, as

Vanderpool conceded: "The pursuit was not, in my opinion, very aggressive. I've seen regimental battalion commanders that would sit by . . . with their maps out under a tent . . . when they should have been up there on the top of the hill seeing what was going on."

Still, he praised the unit's leadership overall, especially at the company level. "I'm inclined to think we had some damn good leadership . . . that's everyone from the commanders down through the non-commissioned officers." Many of the sergeants had ten to twenty years in service. "A lot of our company commanders were former first sergeants, so they were all experienced at the company level," he continued. "We had some really well-trained people. Look at myself, I'd been a former sergeant and now a captain; so, I knew the men, knew what their problems were, and I knew how to make them work; in this case, fight."

Towards the end of the campaign, Jay realized that the Japanese had begun trading space for time. Indeed, they were no longer "defending" Guadalcanal; they were simply fighting a series of "delaying actions" to facilitate their seaborne evacuation. Each day, the Japanese would hold their lines until sunset, and then retreat under the cover of darkness. "The next morning," as Jay described it, "we'd attack in the daylight, and then they'd hold a little bit until dark, and then fall back again. So, it was not a true *pursuit*. It was a series of delaying actions; then on the last night they just held us off until dark, got on the submarines and left. I think that if we would have been more aggressive, we might have knocked off another 1,000 to 1,500 of them."

During their amphibious escape, however, the Japanese had left a few stragglers behind. The Americans had anticipated as much; and as Vanderpool recalled: "We did some patrolling, looking for Jap stragglers. I took advantage of the time to improve our survey system." Land surveying was critical to an artillery officer's mission. It facilitated the timely and accurate delivery of indirect fire support.

During this survey patrol, however, Jay Vanderpool had a near-brush with death.

"I was out supervising some triangulation survey over the terrain we had just taken. We had eight or ten people in the survey party. While climbing over a ridge formerly defended by Japs, I noticed a nicely-constructed bunker. While I was studying the construction details, a Jap that I assumed to be dead jerked his leg out of sight when I accidentally kicked a loose stone in to the hole."

Vanderpool hastily drew his Colt .45.

"Hey boy, come out of that hole!" he bellowed.

The young Japanese soldier was carrying a rifle, a bandolier of ammunition, and four American hand grenades. "I called for some of my men to cover him from the rear," Jay said. "Then, I realized my gun was empty! The ammo clip was back in the glove compartment of my Jeep. My old peacetime training had caused me to unload a gun until I was ready to fire. My arm did some nervous shaking at the thought of an empty gun."

Luckily, the enemy trooper decided not to be a hero; he quickly surrendered.

One of Vanderpool's sergeants confiscated the young man's weapon, and searched him for any pieces of intel. "You should have seen the expression on that Jap kid's face when I loaded my gun back at the Jeep," he chuckled.

"I took him back to Division headquarters for the G-2,"—the Division Intelligence Staff—whereupon he'd be interrogated by Allied counterintelligence specialists. On the way back to Division, however, Jay had a curious run-in with some rear-echelon Marines. "I had to argue with some fat Marine, rear-echelon cooks," he said, "who wanted to kill a Jap."

Vanderpool was dumbfounded.

The battle was over; and these rear-echelon cooks had probably never fired a shot in anger. Yet here they were, begging to shoot an unarmed prisoner as if it were a sporting event. "I recommended they go up in the hills and kill all the *armed* Japs they wanted to. Rear-echelon noncombatants can be quite bloodthirsty. That includes American and Japanese."

For his actions in subduing the enemy soldier, Jay Vanderpool received the Bronze Star Medal. He admitted, however, that if his superior officer had known about the unloaded pistol, he'd have earned a *reprimand* instead of a medal.

According to Vanderpool, the biggest challenges on Guadalcanal had been *communicative* and *logistical.* "The biggest communication problem," he remembered, "was that our primary communications were wire, and all wires were canalized." Indeed, when navigating through the jungle, terrain dictated the availability of maneuver routes. "In so doing, your wires had to follow you," said Vanderpool. The problem, however, was that these field wires were often damaged by tanks, bulldozers, and even wheeled vehicles, thus disabling communications for days. To make matters worse, the terrain did not easily lend itself to digging an underground wire network. After a while, Jay's unit simply began laying down new wires whenever an existing node was damaged. "It was easier and faster just to put in a new wire," he said, "than to find one and repair it."

In terms of logistics: "The biggest problem, I think . . . was the lack of equipment that could cross wet ground." Following a thunderstorm, the river valleys in Guadalcanal would become impenetrable marshlands. Very often, American forces would be in hot pursuit of the Japanese, only to have their advance halted by a river swell.

"It might only be 200 feet wide," said Vanderpool, "but the troops couldn't get across it with their mortar ammunition and things they needed. They had to slow down to get a corduroy road up there, so they could get their supply trucks across to support them when they moved on." As Jay recalled, this was a problem that plagued American forces all throughout the Solomon Islands Campaign—"the problem of soft, muddy . . . marshy roads."

But the fact remained that the US had emerged victorious on Guadalcanal. From that point forward, America would stay on the offensive throughout the Pacific Campaign . . . and the Japanese would grow more desperate to defend their now-fledgling empire.

3

Blood Red Shores

With Guadalcanal secured, the 25th Infantry Division prepared to depart the island. This opening round of the Pacific Campaign had been a decisive victory for Allied forces. Indeed, Guadalcanal had been the first step in the "island hopping" strategy. The goal was to occupy and neutralize certain Japanese-held islands that could strategically support the drive to Tokyo.

On Guadalcanal, "our objective had been taken," said Vanderpool, "and that was to get the airfields, so we just continued our movement on farther north. The airfields were close enough together so that fighters from one island could protect you landing on the next island." But even as they prepared to leave Guadalcanal, the island was still under constant harassment from Japanese bombers. "However, the bombing against our forces was largely ineffective," he recalled. The American occupation force had spread out, "and we put our troops into the woods where they were hard to see." Moreover, the Japanese bombers (particularly the Mitsubishi G4M) were easy prey for Allied fighters like the P-38 Lightning.

On July 21, 1943, "We got a call about 10 o' clock in the morning to start loading the battalion that night to go to New Georgia," said Vanderpool. "One of my jobs was to check the LSTs and some plans for the S-4 [logistics staff] to get them loaded during the night." LSTs were larger landing craft capable of delivering tanks, vehicles, and other equipment simultaneously onto a given beachhead. Unlike the smaller Higgins boats (of D-Day fame), the LSTs were self-contained ships with crew quarters and passenger berths. "We loaded my battalion, the 89th Field Artillery Battalion . . . a little after dark that night." Aboard the LST, however, Jay and his fellow GIs were not merely "passengers." Indeed, aboard every LST, the soldiers were expected to be gainfully employed, helping the ship's company in their critical tasks.

As such, Jay Vanderpool was given charge of the LST's antiaircraft batteries.

Interestingly, however, Jay beefed up the LST's firepower through some creative bartering he had done with the 2d Marine Division on Guadalcanal. As the Marines prepared to leave the island, he noticed they were carrying "a whole bunch of those air-cooled .50 caliber machine guns on pedestals," he said. Walking up to the commander, Jay offered them a trade. "You don't want to carry those heavy damn things back to the re-training areas. Why don't you give them to me?" In exchange for the mounted .50 cals, Vanderpool offered them a couple of extra Jeeps. Because the Marines had lost plenty of Jeeps throughout the campaign, they happily accepted the horse trade. "Anyway," he continued, "we ended up with twelve extra .50 caliber machine guns . . . and I sandbagged [weighted] them all around the perimeter of that ship's deck."

As it turned out, the extra firepower saved the LST's life. Throughout the journey to New Georgia, Vanderpool's convoy was under constant harassment from Japanese aerial patrols. The additional guns aboard his LST, however, dissuaded the enemy attack planes from engaging it—"we put up such a cone of fire, the Japs would go and bomb somebody else. They'd take one look at our cone of fire [the blasting envelope of the aircraft guns], and peel off and hit another ship in the convoy." Sadly, the convoy lost a few LSTs en route to New Georgia but, as Vanderpool admitted, "it really paid dividends, having the most gunfire [aboard his LST] . . . it saved our ship. If the other ships would have had the same number of guns, it might have been different."

Departing Guadalcanal, Jay received an unexpected lateral promotion to Battalion Intelligence Officer (S-2). "The battalion S-2 job," he said, "included survey and the usual intelligence functions, in our case primarily survey, because there were [still] no accurate maps, only uncontrolled photo mosaics. Wherever pictures matched, they were printed. They might be plus or minus 1,000 yards in accuracy. If a cloud went by when you were taking a picture, you could have your objective under a cloud." In the realm of artillery, such obstructions and scaled inaccuracies could be deadly when planning fire missions. Improper distance scaling could lead to misplaced artillery fires, and rounds falling on friendly troops.

But Vanderpool, having been a surveyor (and having taught survey operations to his fellow artillerymen), revitalized the battalion's survey system. "We would traverse into where we were going," he recalled, and subsequently base their surveys off of where the leading infantry elements were located. Based on those reference points, the artillery could then shoot wherever it was needed. "And I think that [ground survey] was one of our biggest contributions in those early campaigns . . . because the infantry didn't know where they were. I know a couple of times the objective was under a cloud on the photo map, and it's hard to locate through a cloud."

The following day, the 89th Field Artillery made landfall on Kokorana Island near Rendova. "We moved our guns ashore to set up a base of fire for the people on the mainland of New Georgia," he said, "which is a few thousand yards away." Kokorana was one of the barrier islands sitting astride the northern coast of Rendova. Although the island measured barely 300 square yards—"just big enough for an artillery battalion"—it offered a great vantage point from which to fire on New Georgia. "All we wanted was a place to set the guns on dry soil and enough space to shoot."

For the landings on New Georgia, the 161st RCT was detached from the 25th Infantry Division, temporarily re-assigned to the 37th Division of the Army National Guard. Their objective was to capture the enemy airfield at Munda Point. The 37th Division, alongside the 43d Division (also of the National Guard) would make a two-pronged attack along the southeastern beaches, maneuvering inland to secure the air strip.

The 89th Field Artillery (still supporting the 161st RCT) then began its preparatory fires onto the coastal hills of New Georgia. On July 25, as the 43d Division pushed along the southern edge of the island to Munda Point, Jay Vanderpool coordinated a barrage of 105mm howitzer fire into the suspected Japanese positions, while nearby Navy destroyers opened fire with their 5-inch deck guns. It was a visually-impressive display of American firepower, but it had little impact on the Japanese occupiers. Indeed, many of the scattered troops reoccupied their bunkers after the prepping fire had lifted.

But when the National Guard made contact with Japanese troops, the American fire support liaisons called for more rounds of crippling fire.

Jay Vanderpool happily obliged.

As the Battalion S-2, he frequently took on additional duties as a Fire Direction Officer, coordinating fire missions for the various howitzer batteries. "I was shooting cannonballs for the National Guard," he said—all of which was going smoothly until the 103d Infantry Regiment (43d Division) got pinned down along the southern end of the island.

As it turned out, the Japanese had planted machine gun teams along a tiny barrier island about 100 yards from the southern coast of the Allied landing site. "The infantry couldn't get to that island on foot;" said Vanderpool, "they didn't have any [tactical] boats and the Japs were out there with machine guns." Indeed, every time the National Guard tried to advance beyond visual range of the Japanese machine guns, "they'd get chewed up," Jay recalled.

"And so, I started shooting at that island."

Jay wasn't about to let a few cleverly-placed machine gunners disrupt the regiment's advance. In fact, Vanderpool delivered so much artillery fire onto that island, he earned the wrath of his battalion commander. "I got hell later," he recalled, "because I just shot so many cannon balls at that one little old island." True, there probably weren't more than two dozen Japanese soldiers manning a total of five machine guns, but this well-concealed nest had "held up the whole flank of a regiment," said Jay. "Anyway, I kept the Japs' heads down for a while, and I must have hurt some of them, because they stopped shooting."

As it turned out, he was correct.

The Americans recovered several dead enemy troops from that barrier island.

With the machine gunners now silenced, the National Guardsmen broke loose from their tactical chokepoint and captured the airfield at Munda Point.

On the heels of the National Guardsmen came a US Naval construction battalion (the ubiquitous "Seabees," as they were called). "The Seabees were right behind us with their bulldozers and airfield building equipment," Jay continued. "They went ashore so they could put in an airfield,"—supplemental to the enemy airstrip at Munda that the Allies had just captured. "It was to get another fighter field up there, so we could then launch to protect our landings up farther north in Bougainville and places like Rabaul." As Vanderpool recalled, the area surrounding Munda was ideal for such an airstrip. "The soil was decomposed coral and limestone," he said, "which makes for a beautiful runway." In fact, Jay compared these coral-based runways to the granite-based airfields he later saw in Vietnam. "Decomposed granite," he said, "was very similar; it was very fine and once you mounded and packed it, it was almost like concrete. It made a beautiful runway, and you could build it with a few bulldozers and graders. You could knock out a runway before you knew it."

Aside from the Seabees' remarkable craftsmanship, Jay also praised them for their tactical ingenuity. For when the Seabees arrived on the beach (500 yards behind the advancing infantry), each of their bulldozers had a rifleman perched atop the crossarm of the dozer blade. "When the Japs would pop out of a hole," said Jay, "three or four bulldozers with riflemen aboard would move over and shoot at them. Then they'd go on pushing coral around."

A few days later, the 89th Field Artillery Battalion came ashore at New Georgia. And just as before, the 89th was rendering fire support to the 161st RCT. By now, the fledgling Japanese had occupied the hills north of Munda Point; and the Americans were determined to pry the enemy from the high ground. "With the Japs on that hill mass," said Vanderpool, they could shoot down into the field [Munda airstrip], which discouraged the pilots." But after only three days of concentrated artillery fire, Vanderpool's howitzer batteries had successfully blasted the enemy off the hill.

The Japanese, meanwhile, had sent a Special Naval Landing Forces detachment to the shores of Bairoko, about 20 miles north of Munda Point. These "Special Naval Landing Forces" were, in essence, Japanese Marines. "They had amphibious people, infantry, artillery, all the services . . . it was a miniature task force." And, as it were, this naval infantry force was headed south to interdict American forces near the Munda airfield.

Little did the Japanese know, however, that they were walking into a trap.

"To me, the only good artillery target I ever shot in my entire military career," said Jay, "was at that time." US Naval intelligence had reported the Japanese landings . . . and that they were headed straight for the American positions south near Munda Point. The jungle canopy, however, had concealed their inland movements from aerial observation. "We knew they were down in the woods somewhere . . . but we didn't know where [exactly]."

As a precaution, however, Jay Vanderpool registered one howitzer from *each* battalion in the XIV Corps Artillery onto the crossroads leading into Munda Airfield from the north. These crossroads, as they were, converged onto a big clearing "which must have been three or four hundred yards in diameter with woods north of it," said Vanderpool.

As luck would have it, the Japanese naval infantry came blithering out of the woods, right onto the crossroads where Jay had aimed the corps' artillery. The members of this Special Naval Landing Force were "dirty, smelly, wet, hungry, and tired"—exhausted from their trek across the wetland jungles. "They had been stomping through that mud for three or four days," said Vanderpool. "When they got to the clearing, the first thing they did was take off their shirts and wring out their clothes." The Japanese troops then took off their boots and began wringing their socks. "Meanwhile, Japs just kept coming, and coming, and still coming out of the woods."

Jay Vanderpool was ecstatic.

This was *the* best target grouping he could imagine.

And the Japanese had no idea they were under direct observation from American artillery.

"I kept wanting to shoot but thought, 'No, I'll hold a little longer.' I had every artillery piece available within the corps, say five or six battalions . . . all just registered within an hour before, so I just sat there and waited and waited."

Jay wanted to kill as many Japanese troops in the open as possible.

"Finally, I just couldn't wait any longer. I called for a TOT, time on target. So, here they came . . . five or six battalions, TOT, all burst within a few seconds of one another, right in the middle of this assembly area in the open."

The Japanese panicked.
In the clearing, there wasn't one blade of grass or shrubbery to hide behind. Thus, the fiery shrapnel of the 105mm rounds tore through the Japanese with a primitive fury. "We continued this fire for 10 or 20 minutes," Vanderpool recalled. "Then, I raised the fire and pushed it inland, into the woods about a half-mile."

He didn't want the Japanese to escape.

Spastically running back into the jungle, the shell-shocked survivors of the initial barrage were violently cut down by the adjusted fire.

Thirty minutes after Vanderpool ended the fire mission, the 161st RCT sent a scout team into the jungle one mile beyond the clearing. As Jay grimly recalled, that immediate patch of jungle "was piled up with dead Japs, plus the several hundred that were down in the clearing."

Reflecting on this target-rich opportunity, Vanderpool concluded that the Japanese must have had poor intelligence regarding the Americans' whereabouts, or the reach of their indirect fires. "I don't think they knew we had the airfield," he said. "They'd been up there in the woods for several days, sloshing around in that knee-deep mud, kicking their shins on those old roots. They were happy just to get out of those damn woods, get out in the fresh air and dry out a little bit." And when these Japanese naval troops emerged from the woods, they were too exhausted to realize that the Americans had occupied the high ground, with coordinated artillery fires at the ready.

As the Allies moved farther inland, the 27th Infantry Regiment (25th Infantry Division) came ashore with the mission of advancing north towards Zieta and Bairoko—"that's where the Jap Marines, or Special Naval Landing parties, had come from," said Jay. Meanwhile, the 89th Field Artillery (now rendering fire support to the 27th Regiment) began to coordinate their target points.

But here again, the photo-based maps were problematic.

"We weren't sure where the trail to Zieta village was," said Vanderpool. Looking at the photo mosaics, however, he identified a terrain feature that he deduced to be the Zieta Trail. During the next pre-mission brief, the 27th Infantry's regimental commander turned to Vanderpool and said:

"Van, is this the trail?" pointing to the faint, winding structure depicted on the photo.

"Yes sir, that's the trail."

"How do you know?"

"That looks like the trail to me; that's where the Japs came out."

Indeed, the outline on the photo mosaic generally followed the point where the ill-fated Japanese Marines had emerged from the jungle . . . and into Vanderpool's kill zone. If nothing else, following the trail would lead them to the Japanese Marines' initial staging area. For this operation up the Zieta Trail, Jay volunteered to accompany the 27th Infantry Regiment as a fire support liaison.

But when the 27th Infantry began its drive along the Zieta Trail, they ran into an immediate delaying action from the Japanese; the enemy had set up defensive positions approximately every 500 yards.

No surprises here, Vanderpool thought.

After the Japanese Marines had been cut down so viciously near Munda, he expected the enemy to place some residual defenses along the routes into Bairoko. From their volume of fire, however, Vanderpool estimated that the Japanese had a battalion-sized element stretched across the jungle—"and their reserves were probably still coming up," he added. But after seeing the regimental advance halted *twice* by the Japanese defenders, Vanderpool decided to call for the dreaded "sound-and-fragment" artillery.

To accomplish the sound-and-fragment fire, "you'd shoot a volley in front of you a ways, then walk it back slowly." Then, whenever the farthest-forward friendly troops could see the shell fragments arcing back towards their friendly lines, the artillery's Forward Observers would signal the howitzers to hold that firing position without further adjustment. "You'd listen to the sound of the incoming rounds," he explained, "and pull the fire back until the tail-spray [i.e., fragments from the backblast of the shell's impact] went over your head. Then that's as close as you could get." In other words, the Forward Observers would tell the batteries how close they could bring their cannon fire without committing fratricide.[7] "The Infantry didn't like this," he admitted, "because the tail-spray fragments went all over their area whenever we pulled it back that close; but if you didn't have [the artillery fire] that close, it wouldn't do you *any* good in close fighting."

At some point, while Vanderpool was adjusting the sound-and-fragment fire, he recalled that: "Someone had a bright idea that the infantry would fall back two hundred or three hundred yards and let the artillerymen stay out in front." Unbeknownst to Jay, someone at the regiment had decided to let the artillery liaisons adjust their fires all alone, "then the infantry would come back up and take the ground." Thus, Jay and his half-dozen artillerymen were now the forward-most element of the Division's advance.

However, as Jay continued rolling back his artillery fire, the Japanese suddenly realized that the American lines had de-populated. "So, they decided to counterattack," said Jay. "They could see that there weren't very many of us." As he recalled, the Japanese were closing to within thirty yards of the American line—"sneaking around trees like Indians and shooting at us."

With the enemy that close, there was only one option left.

The Americans would have to register artillery fire *on their own position.*

Lieutenant Colonel John Ferris, the senior-ranking officer on the line, turned to Vanderpool and said:

"Van, we're going to stop them!"

With that, Ferris keyed the radio: "Drop 100!"

"This put the volley right square on top of us," Jay recalled.

"We called maximum rate of fire for 20 minutes . . . because the Japs were all around us by this time. We had one battalion of light 105s, one battalion of medium 155s, right on top of us for 20 minutes. Of course, you could hear [the shells] coming when you shoot high angle-of-fire. We kept this up until the Japs stopped." After the surviving Japanese pulled back, the 27th Infantry Regiment passed through the beleaguered artillerymen, on to the next objective along the Zieta Trail. "Johnny Ferris got the Silver Star," said Vanderpool, "for calling fire on top of ourselves to stop the Jap attack."

Securing Zieta (and the surrounding vicinity) was the last major battle on New Georgia. "There was a lot of mopping up and skirmishing around," he said. But after linking up with the Marines at Barioko: "We went back to Guadalcanal for staging on transports back to New Zealand, to get the men back into a healthier climate, and put a little fat on them, and get them in condition to restart another training program."

Resting and refitting were an important part of a unit's combat cycle. It allowed time for soldiers to decompress from the horrors of combat, enjoy some leisure time, and continue training for the next combat operation. Then, too, many soldiers had to recover from the normal variety of tropical diseases—malaria, dysentery, cholera, and dengue fever. Vanderpool referred to the latter ailment as "breakbone fever," calling it the "worst fever I've ever had." While most of the tropical ailments could be resolved with just a few days' medical care, Jay saw many of his comrades succumb to the ravages of malaria. This mosquito-borne infection was the "silent killer" for many a GI serving in the Pacific or the China-Burma-India theater.

Arriving in New Zealand, the 25th Division enjoyed the first long break they had seen since Guadalcanal. "Every morning for breakfast we had steak and eggs, and had a pitcher of beer on one end of the table for the old-timers, a pitcher of milk on the other end for the recruits. Everyone ate and drank whatever he wanted starting at breakfast." Most of the soldiers were young men—"kids, you know, in their early twenties"—said Vanderpool. And he admired how quickly they could bounce back from the stresses of combat.

It was now the fall of 1943, and the US had been at war for nearly two years. The Allied victories at Midway, Guadalcanal, and New Georgia added to the momentum of the Pacific Campaign. Meanwhile, on the other side of the world, Allied Forces were making similar progress against Nazi Germany and Fascist Italy. After some initial setbacks in North Africa, the Americans had regained the initiative, dismantling Erwin Rommel's *Afrika Korps* and establishing a base from which to invade Italy and Sicily. From these developments, it seemed that the war was turning in the Allies' favor.

After a few months' rest in New Zealand, the 25th Division went to New Caledonia for what Vanderpool called an "intensive training cycle." Before departing New Zealand, however, the Division received an influx of replacements—new recruits and draftees reporting for duty—"plus an overstrength," he recalled, as a pre-emptive backfill for early casualties. "We went into a training cycle, starting off with company, battalion, and Division exercises. As soon as we got through the cycles, we'd turn around and run through them again, now teaching them to fight in open terrain. You see, our men had never fought in the open and they had little concept of maneuver in the open." New Caledonia was the ideal terrain for such maneuvers—"open country, rolling hills . . . nothing out there but a lot of deer and not many natives."

As their training cycle continued, Jay wondered aloud where the 25th Division would go next. "It might have been Halmahera

[Indonesia]; it might have been the Philippines; it might have been Borneo . . . we didn't know." But wherever the next combat operations might be, Jay Vanderpool would experience it from a different vantage point. Indeed, while still on New Caledonia, he was released from the 89th Field Artillery Battalion and reassigned to Division Headquarters. "There was a vacancy in the Division G-2 section [Intelligence staff]," he said. The Division Intelligence Officer, Lieutenant Colonel Rob Stevenson (descendant of the famous author Robert Lewis Stevenson) had made a by-name request for Jay Vanderpool to be transferred onto his staff.

At first, Jay didn't know what to make of the sudden reassignment. He had performed his duties well, but he didn't think that his performance warranted attention from the Division-level headhunters. "The selection," as he found out, "resulted from a school I had attended between campaigns on Guadalcanal [in 1942]." Admiral William Halsey, commander of the South Pacific Area, had established a joint training program on "combat scouting and patrolling." The course drew officers from every branch of US service. "Instructors were from all services, plus [Australian] Coastwatchers and Malayan Scouts. We were taught scouting, map reading, sketching, 'jungle medicine,' bivouac construction, 'pidgin English,' and compass navigation. As a graduation exercise, we were required to move by platoon-sized units across the mountain ranges of Guadalcanal."

It was strange that Admiral Halsey would choose to establish a training course on Guadalcanal in 1942, when American forces were still trying to wrest the island from Japanese control. But such was the supposed "urgency" of the course and its topics. If the student patrols encountered any Japanese troops along the way, they were authorized to kill or capture the enemy accordingly. Jay led one patrol, wherein he was given a "composite platoon of many services and ranks." They did not encounter any Japanese during the course of their training, but: "When we finished those patrols, a secret written ballot that I knew nothing about, was taken. I was elected the outstanding patrol leader."

Hence, the reason for his selection by the Division G-2.

Lieutenant Colonel Stevenson saw the value of having a staff officer with expert knowledge of scouting and patrolling.

"One of the hardest things to teach American kids in those days," said Vanderpool, "was that the jungle was not going to eat you." Essentially, the Pacific jungles weren't much different from the woods in North America. The biggest differences were the types of wildlife and the quantities of rainfall. "The main thing is to learn how to survive out there and not get sick. How to take care of your feet; how to rest your troops before they become casualties." Thus, Jay took it upon himself to teach his classmates the art of survivalism. "I taught them how to make a fire [particularly in a wet environment], how to set up a lean-to, how to dry out their clothes at night . . . little things like that." Jay also taught them the importance of resting on high ground after crossing a river. "When you have to cross a river," he said, "don't stop down in the river valley and let everyone's muscles get cold so they can't climb; but take onto the next ridge, then let them stop and take a break." Indeed, most of his classmates in the patrolling course (and most of the incoming soldiers) had never lived in the woods or the mountains. "It was a whole new environment to them," he said.

He credited his success in the patrolling course to his rough and rural upbringing. "As a kid, I lived in New Mexico, Arizona . . . the plains country, and in the mountains all my life. My parents didn't worry about me. I could go walking and camping with nothing but my dog and a rifle. I was raised learning how to make fire, keep warm, and how to stay dry in wet weather. This really paid dividends in teaching other people how to do it. A lot of these kids off the sidewalk don't have that training. They probably don't have it today, except for those lucky few that have had Boy Scout training."

But unlike the Boy Scout training program, "ours was *survival* scouting," he said, "because out there in the Solomons, we were all living out in the open."

Arriving at Division Headquarters, Jay was promoted to major within the week. "It was one of those on-the-job promotion things," he said. But as Jay Vanderpool settled into his new role as a Division staff officer, he received a curious communique from the Southwest Pacific Area Headquarters.

They were soliciting volunteers for a "highly hazardous" mission.

4

Behind Enemy Lines

By the spring of 1944, American forces in the South Pacific had been re-assigned to a new theater-level command—the Southwest Pacific Area (SWPA). Commanded by General Douglas MacArthur, SWPA was committed to retaking the Philippine Islands and facilitating the drive to Tokyo. For General MacArthur, however, the mission to retake the Philippines was personal. Two years earlier, he had fled the Philippines in the wake of the Allied surrender on Bataan, vowing famously "I shall return."

An American Commonwealth since 1898, the Philippine Islands had been transitioning to full sovereignty since the mid-1930s. Indeed, the Tydings-McDuffie Act of 1935 had authorized a ten-year timeline for Philippine independence. By the time of its ratification, however, Tydings-McDuffie was little more than a formality—the Philippines had been virtually autonomous for years. They elected their own leaders, made their own laws in the Philippine Assembly, conducted free trade with other nations, and enjoyed the full protection of the United States military. American forces in the Philippines fell under the jurisdiction of the United States Armed Forces—Far East (USAFFE)[1]. Commanded by an Army General, USAFFE encompassed all US military assets in the Philippine archipelago. This included American ground forces,

---

[1] Pronounced "You-SAW-fee."

the Far East Air Force, the Asiatic Fleet, and the semi-autonomous Philippine Army. USAFFE's mission was simple: continue providing combat-capable units for the Commonwealth's defense and assume responsibility for training the Philippine Army until the Islands achieved full independence.

Despite these mission parameters, however, USAFFE had suffered under the same draconian defense budgets that had plagued Vanderpool's unit in Hawaii. USAFFE, much like the latter-day Hawaiian Division, perennially subsisted on less than half of the men and equipment it needed for its missions.

Thus, it came as no surprise when, on the morning of December 8, 1941, the American-Philippine contingent found themselves woefully outgunned and outnumbered against the Japanese invasion force.[8] By the following April, the Americans had been pushed back to the Bataan Peninsula and Corregidor Island. Realizing their situation was untenable, the American-Philippine forces reluctantly surrendered to the wrath of the Rising Sun.

Most of the surrendering troops found themselves on the Bataan Death March. A few, however, chose not to surrender. These daring souls—including Russell Volckmann, Donald Blackburn, Wendell Fertig, and Robert Lapham—disappeared into the jungle and raised guerrilla movements against the Japanese. By 1943, the guerrillas operating in North Luzon had established radio contact with MacArthur's new headquarters in Australia—soliciting supplies, providing intelligence on Japanese troop dispositions, and seeking liaisons to facilitate operations with Allied conventional forces.

"We got a message at one time during the summer," said Jay, "from GHQ, SWPA, MacArthur's headquarters. They were asking for each division to nominate one officer of field grade rank [major and above] to volunteer for a highly hazardous program. The requirements were all the good characteristics of Boy Scouts, plus combat experience in the field . . . a long list of fine attributes a person had to have."

Normally, Vanderpool's boss, Colonel Stevenson would be the one to handle requests from higher headquarters, but: "Stevenson was in the hospital with malaria or something," Jay recalled, "and I was the acting G-2." Thus, Jay Vanderpool began scouring the ranks of the division, looking for the best-qualified men based on SWPA's parameters. "Patrolling was one of the things I loved to do anyway," he admitted. "I scoured and scoured, and finally came up with the two best-qualified people—Dick Ferriter and myself. And for various reasons, I deduced that I was better qualified than Dick. Dick should maybe stay behind in the recon troop." In fact, while serving with the Division's reconnaissance company, Dick Ferriter would later earn the Distinguished Service Cross.[9]

Despite nominating himself for the position, Vanderpool's self-selection was approved, and he was given orders to Hollandia, New Guinea, where the SWPA Headquarters had just relocated. Upon his arrival, Jay recalled a series of intense, whirlwind briefings, all of which were given by Colonels Court Whitney and Steve Melnick. Both men worked for General Charles Willoughby, MacArthur's chief of intelligence.[10] "Although General Willoughby didn't personally conduct the briefings, except for the final sendoffs," said Jay, "he monitored the selection of people, and the training they got, prior to going in. We had a number of people who were then working with the guerrillas in the Philippines, general intelligence types. They briefed us on the terrain, the enemy situation, etc."

Oddly enough, Jay and his comrades were forbidden to take notes during the briefing.

"It was a memory cram," he said. "No examination, but they didn't want a bunch of secret notes scattered around the theater." Vanderpool appreciated the concern, but there was only so much information one could hold in their short-term memory.

Still, the briefings were an adventure unto themselves. Jay and his comrades were genuinely impressed by the progress their comrades had made on the guerrilla front. Despite the normal growing pains associated with raising guerrilla forces, many of the Allied partisans had made considerable headway against the Japanese occupiers, slowly attriting enemy forces and disrupting their supply networks. By this point, one of the most well-organized guerrilla units was the "United States Armed Forces in the Philippines—North Luzon" (USAFIP-NL), a regimental-sized unit commanded by Colonel Russ Volckmann. USAFIP-NL had been organized from among the various Philippine Army units that were scattered behind enemy lines as the Japanese moved southward to Bataan. Other notable guerrilla units included the Luzon Guerrilla Army Force (LGAF) commanded by Robert Lapham in Southern Luzon, and James Cushing's guerrillas on the island of Cebu. The Allied partisans now wanted to coordinate their guerrilla operations with friendly conventional forces to facilitate the enemy's destruction.

"After a few weeks of intensive briefings," Jay continued, "we were given our missions." As it turned out, Jay's mission was to infiltrate North Luzon, by submarine, at Lingayen Gulf—"and offload a team of people to work with Colonel Volckmann and other American guerrilla leaders, so that when our own divisions arrived, we'd have people oriented on the terrain and the enemy situation." As Jay recalled, many of these early infiltrators were Assistant G-2s from the various Army divisions in the Pacific.

"All of them had several campaigns under their belts," he added.

"In my patrol, we had a Major George Miller from a California National Guard outfit; we had two lieutenants, plus meteorological experts to setup weather stations in the interior [mountains of Luzon], some demolition men, and some radio operators, code clerks . . . all highly skilled technicians. We were all assigned a submarine to drive us to the Philippines. We drew the [USS] *Cero* . . . which was one of the older models, but a good submarine."

For their voyage into the Philippines, however, the Navy removed many of the *Cero*'s torpedoes, which gave Vanderpool's team the cargo space they needed to accommodate the 17 tons of supplies they were bringing ashore. But Jay and his team of commandos, unfazed by the partial disarmament of their submarine, went straight to work . . . lining the bulkheads with "weapons, ammunition, radios, batteries, medical supplies, whatever the people back at base thought the guerrilla forces could use." And, as Jay admitted, the cargo tonnage "didn't leave very much room. There was only about three to four feet of space on top of that pile for the men to ride."

Setting sail in September 1944, the Vanderpool commandos headed north to the Philippine archipelago. "We weren't afraid so much of the Japanese aircraft [or enemy subs]," said Jay, "but we *were* afraid of American aircraft. The depth charges the Japanese aircraft carried were not considered to be really dangerous to the type of sub I was on. However, the American depth charges could sink you." Sadly, fratricide (and near-fratricide) had become a recurring problem between Allied aircraft and naval vessels. Of late, the Army Air Force pilots in-theater had become increasingly trigger-happy against enemy subs. "A pilot can't tell one black submarine from another black submarine when it's cruising along on the surface; they all look alike," Jay recalled. "That was our biggest worry. Almost daily, American bombers out on patrol spotted us, or we spotted them. We had several bombers make runs at us. But none ever got close enough to put a depth charge within a half-mile of us, because we could dive, turn, and get away."

Other Allied subs weren't so lucky.

Indeed, the following month, a USAAF bomber accidentally sank an American submarine while the latter was en route to deliver supplies to Russell Volckmann's guerrillas in North Luzon.

"So, we chugged on up through the islands between New Guinea and the Philippines," Jay continued. "It's the first time I'd ever been on a submarine, and I loved it. It was a lot of fun and the food was good. It was comfortable and warm." He added, half-jokingly, that a soldier could earn a degree in hydrological engineering simply by learning to flush a submarine's toilet when submerged at 300 feet.

Aside from their occasional "close calls" with overzealous Allied bombers, Vanderpool's submarine also had a close encounter with the "Singapore Fleet" of the Imperial Japanese Navy. "We were off the coast due west of Mindoro," he said, when the radar detected the entire fleet headed in their direction. "I believe there were four or five battleships, several heavy cruisers and light cruisers, and a whole passel of destroyers and destroyer escorts."

By this point in the war, it was the last big surface fleet in the Japanese Navy.

"In our mission orders," said Jay, "the submarine commander had to have my permission to attack [enemy vessels]." As leader of the patrol landing party, Jay Vanderpool was given authority to determine whether a potential target at sea was of higher priority than the mission to deliver the SWPA commandos to Lingayen Gulf. And although the *Cero* was underway with far fewer torpedoes than it normally carried, the sub commander nevertheless asked Jay for permission to engage. Jay's answer was simple:

"Hell yes! If we get one of those battleships, it's well paid for . . . that's all profit!"

Vectoring the submarine due west, Vanderpool watched with delight as the USS *Cero* drew closer towards weapons envelope with the leading Japanese ship. But as their submarine closed within 10 miles of the enemy armada, "they split the fleet," he said wryly. "The battleships went south . . . and the other ships went northeast. We never got within torpedo range." Still, these elusive enemy vessels would later meet their demise during the Battle of Leyte Gulf. Watching helplessly as the Japanese fleet steamed out of firing range, Jay vectored the submarine captain back onto their original course for Lingayen Gulf.

"We got up to Lingayen," he said, "where I was supposed to unload and join a US Army Colonel Volckmann. But there was some confusion. The Japanese were unloading three or four infantry divisions over the beach at San Fernando del Norte, our destination [on the shores of Lingayen Gulf]."

Frustrated by the sudden arrival of enemy troops, Vanderpool had little choice but to wait offshore aboard the *Cero* and see what the Japanese did next. "So, we just watched and tried to figure what to do next, because we couldn't go in there." Indeed, there were thousands of Japanese soldiers going over the beach. Vanderpool radioed SWPA Headquarters, asking for guidance. "We laid out there overnight," he recalled, "waiting for an answer to 'What's next, Coach?'"

The following morning, HQ sent their answer.

SWPA ordered Vanderpool to guide the submarine around the northern tip of the island, across the Luzon Strait to the Philippine Sea, and then down along the eastern coast of Luzon—where Army Air Force Major Bernard Anderson had a guerrilla camp (and a comms station) north of Infanta. "Anderson would help us unload the submarine," he said, "then from there we'd get new instructions. Of course, the Navy would be happy to get us off their submarine so they could get back to work; and we would be happy to get back on the beach."

But as the USS *Cero* rounded its way across the northern coast, and into the Babuyan Channel, Vanderpool got his first taste of a close-quarters depth charge salvo. "We were cruising north on the surface, one or two miles offshore at night, when we encountered a small 3,000–4,000-ton Jap freighter headed south," he recalled.

But Vanderpool noticed something peculiar about this freighter.

The bridge looked horribly misshapen. As if it had been blown apart.

"We could see it clearly through the periscope," he said.

"Apparently, some American [plane or vessel] had shot or bombed away her entire forecastle structure." Aside from the collapsing bridge, she appeared to be sinking at the bow—"water was slopping across the deck and breaking around the bridge." Moreover, this out-of-place Japanese freighter had no naval escort in sight. "She was not really worth a torpedo," said Jay, and most of the available torpedo tubes were still occupied by the guerrilla's cargo.

Still, this freighter was flying the enemy's flag. And it likely had wartime materiel on board. Thus, when the *Cero*'s commander requested to open fire with the submarine's deck guns, Vanderpool approved the request. "In those days submarine deck guns were manned by the cooks and kitchen people," he said. "The captain thought it would be fun to let the cooks go on deck to man the bow gun and the twin 20mm automatic anti-aircraft guns. The cooks and mess attendants were delighted. They normally do not have much chance to shoot at anyone."

Loading the forward battery, the submarine crept to within a quarter-mile before opening fire on the ailing steamship. "The bow gun soon had two or three hits," Jay recalled. The combination of 20mm tracer and incendiary bullets soon ignited an oil fire aboard the deck. "The Japanese skipper took his brightly burning vessel on the beach,"—a desperate attempt to save the ship by running it aground.

But this incendiary detour with the Japanese freighter turned out to be more trouble than it was worth.

For within minutes, the *Cero*'s radar team reported "several surface vessels" closing in from the north at flank speed." Indeed, the firepower jaunt against the freighter had gotten the attention of a nearby task force of Japanese destroyers. "We learned later that the [Japanese freighter] was the last survivor of a convoy bringing reinforcements to the Philippines. The other freighter transports had already been sunk by US ships or aircraft. Our target had had plenty of time to send out a plea for help." Since the Japanese destroyers had no one left to "escort" they gladly turned their attention onto Vanderpool's submarine.

"We turned out to sea to get some deeper water," he said, "dived and pretended we were not there." Around this time, the submarine captain identified their pursuers as four *Chidori*-class destroyers. "These were small, shallow draft vessels with pretty good deck guns," said Jay. "The shallow draft made them hard to torpedo. Their main batteries far outgunned our submarines and they carried a lot of depth charges, as we soon confirmed."

Diving to more than 300 feet, the *Cero* searched for a layer of cold water in which to hide. One of the oldest tricks in submarine warfare was to find varying water temperatures, which tended to deflect sonar detection signals. Unfortunately, the *Cero* wouldn't find a shelf of cold water until the following day. Thus, in the meantime, the four angry destroyers dropped their entire arsenal of depth charges while chasing Vanderpool's sub. "This they did with great enthusiasm and wanton disregard of the Japanese Empire's current shortage of munitions." The *Chidori*-class vessels took up a rectangular formation, each occupying one corner of the rectangle as a "sonar position" while estimating that the Cero was somewhere within their sonar field. "The four ships would 'ping' us," Jay continued, "and give our location to a fifth [ship] who would cruise above us and drop a stick of depth charges. Given the acoustics, Vanderpool deduced that each of the ships were taking turns dropping charges and occupying sonar stations.

"You could hear the growling of the engines, the threshing of the propellers overhead, and the rhythmic concussion waves of the depth charges as they approached and faded away. When the charges got real close, you listened after each one to detect any sound of incoming water. My station was the officers' wardroom where I stayed the rest of that night and most of the next day. We were using the air trapped in the submarine to save oxygen for an emergency. The air was so poor you had to light your cigarette while the match was flaring as there was not enough oxygen for wood to burn. I had heard artillery and bombs at close range, but depth charges against a metal hull gave a different sound—no more sinister, but different."

At daybreak the following morning, the *Cero* slipped beneath a shelf of colder water, thus robbing the destroyers of their critical sonar signals. As the *Chidori*-class vessels ended their pursuit, the sound of charge blasts fell farther into the distance. "After dark we surfaced, pumped in some fresh air and started re-charging the batteries and continued on our mission." The captain then invited

Vanderpool on deck for some fresh air. With a comical grin, the captain asked him regarding the depth-charge attack:

"What did you think of that?"

"I'm glad you were signed for this US Government submarine and not me," Jay replied.

"So, we chugged around northern Luzon to the east coast, and met Anderson and his party after dark. This was by pre-arranged signals—flashlights. He helped us unload using canoes before daylight,"—after which the USS *Cero* returned to sea.

Wading ashore to Bernard Anderson's camp, Jay Vanderpool and his team spent the next two weeks awaiting their next instructions from SWPA. "In the meantime," he said, "we were getting a little accli-mated to the weather. We talked to the guerrillas. They had a lot of intelligence reports coming in, which we helped to edit, and tried to do a little collating where we could." Jay was impressed by Anderson's unit—calling it a "fine organization." He noted, however, that Anderson's guerrillas were not *combat* troops, but more akin to spies and field agents. "It was almost purely intelligence and sabotage- type work," said Jay. "He had contact with a lot of combat units, of course, but he didn't run any himself; he wanted to stay on the other side of the business."

A few days later, Anderson's radio terminal finally received a communique from MacArthur's headquarters. Addressed to Jay Vanderpool, the message simply read:

Vanderpool from MacArthur:
Do what you think will best further the Allied cause.

"It's about as broad a directive as they could give a 27-year-old major," Vanderpool laughed. "So, with that in mind, I talked to

Anderson some and analyzed where all the other Americans worked. They had radio stations, so we knew where they were located and talked to them almost daily."

Jay noticed, however, that there were no Americans operating in the area south of Manila Bay and southwest of Manila. "There had been one [American] just north of there," Jay recalled, "but something happened to him." Jay was likely referring to LTC Claude Thorpe, a USAFFE provost marshal who was (nominally) in charge of the earliest guerrilla factions in Luzon. Thorpe, however, had quickly run afoul of the other guerrilla movements—particularly the *Hukbalahap*, an amalgamated militia of the Philippine Socialist and Communist Parties. Thorpe was captured by the Japanese in October 1942.

All in all, Jay knew that if the Americans wanted to retake the Philippines, they would need an American liaison to the guerrilla units operating in and around the capital city. "There were a number of promising guerrilla units over there," he said . . . but one guerrilla unit in particular had caught his attention:

The Hunters ROTC Guerrillas.

Most of its members had been cadets at the Philippine Military Academy (PMA) when the Japanese invaded. When the Japanese made landfall in Luzon, the PMA Classes of 1942 and 1943 were hastily given their commissions and told to fight the invaders. The 300 junior-ranking cadets in the Classes of 1944 and 1945, however, were told to go home; the PMA leadership had determined they were "too young" to die in the war. With that, the PMA dissolved itself for the duration of the conflict. Undeterred, however, the newly-dismissed underclassmen formed their own guerrilla unit, determined to resist the enemy by whatever means possible.

Aside from the young displaced cadets, the Hunters ROTC included many younger PMA graduates, and Philippine Army officers who had attended West Point or Annapolis. "There were many former sergeants and captains from the Philippine Scouts," Jay added. The Philippine Scouts were considered the "elite" of the islands' indigenous forces. They were an American Army unit whose junior officers and enlisted members were entirely Filipino. Given the breadth of military experience within their ranks, the ROTC guerrillas were perhaps the best-trained and well-organized guerrilla outfits in their area. "It was ideologically-oriented at the top," he said, "and had good professional training at the lower ranks in the company grades." Indeed, most Filipinos were decidedly pro-American. They vastly preferred their US affiliation over the heavy-handed brutality of the Japanese.

"We sent couriers on ahead of us, and I went out pretty heavily-laden, going west right across the mountains to get to Laguna de Bay"—the vast lake bordering the southeastern edge of Manila. "It took a few days to get across those mountains, heavy radios and code gear, plus a few medical supplies, extra guns and ammunition." As Vanderpool described it, this hardware was exactly the kind of "trading material" one would need when interacting with guerrillas. "You could give them some guns and ammunition and medical supplies, and you were bound to be welcome."

Getting these supplies to the guerrillas without drawing attention from the enemy, however, was certain to be a task unto itself.

Heading south, the first leg of Vanderpool's journey into Laguna de Bay began along the coastal skerries of Infanta. Rowing his canoes around the peninsula, he intended to make landfall at the southern end of Infanta, hitting the trails that paralleled either Highway 6 or the Famy-Real-Infanta Road. "The Japs had a few hundred men stationed there [along the southern peninsula of Infanta] with some patrol boats," said Jay.

Hardly a promising start.

But Mother Nature came to the rescue.

For on that day, the far edge of a typhoon came blasting through the area.

"Winds must have been 30, 40, or 50 miles an hour," he recalled—which was enough to dissuade the Japanese from running their cyclic patrols. "We knew the Japs weren't going out . . . in that rough weather, in their small boats," he continued. "So, we got a big banca [canoe], a huge one, and we loaded everyone into this big old canoe. It didn't look too seaworthy, but it looked better than meeting those Japanese patrol boats with guns on them."

That night, under the cover of darkness and torrential rains, Jay Vanderpool and his team of commandos, navigated the choppy waters aboard their oversized canoe. Luckily, the storm blew itself out by daylight, allowing the soaked operators to come ashore without incident. "We wanted to start across the mountains," he said, but the group decided to set up camp for a day, allowing their clothes and equipment to dry. "Then we moved in about ten miles to get off the beach and get our stuff rearranged." To affect their journey into the wilderness, and stay away from the Japanese-controlled thoroughfares, Jay hired a group of local tribesmen to guide them across the mountainous terrain. "They were the mountain people," said Vanderpool, the native tribal inhabitants of the Philippine Islands. As Vanderpool described them, they were: "about five foot tall, very dark skin, wiry and agile . . . and strong." In fact, the tribal chieftain himself accompanied Vanderpool's men on the journey—acting as their guide and primary hunter. "His daughter was my pack carrier," said Jay; "after the patrol was over, I very graciously gave her an undershirt for a dress, because she didn't have a dress. She had a fiber skirt made out of grass. She was eternally grateful for her first piece of western clothing."

At some point during their journey, Vandepool's commandos rendezvoused with a field rep from the ROTC guerrillas—a Major Lazo. He worked directly for Colonel Eluterio "Terry" Adevoso, a co-founder and current commander of the Hunters ROTC. Lazo helped guide Vanderpool and his men towards the Hunters ROTC territory. Within sight of Laguna de Bay, Vanderpool and his team went into a nighttime bivouac, taking shelter in an old Catholic Church. "The Japanese were using the road along the east coast of [Laguna de Bay] during the night, hiding out during the day, so American bombers and fighter planes couldn't find them," Jay recalled.

Once inside the church, the parish priest took Vanderpool up to the belfry suite. Ironically, this boarding arrangement would soon save Vanderpool's life. The belfry tower suite was where the local nuns resided. "The [church] bells were above the rooms," said Jay. "I went up and sat in the belfry, trying to keep a low profile until it got dark." He survived the night without issue. But at daybreak, two Japanese infantry companies came barging into the sanctuary. Unaware that a team of American commandos were on the premises, the Japanese troops set up their own bivouac on the ground floor of the church—"sleeping on the pews and cooking out in the yard."

At first, Jay didn't panic.

Perhaps the Japanese would enjoy their temporary bivouac and leave without searching the upper levels of the church. But as fate would have it, one of the Japanese officers wanted to come upstairs.

Now, Jay was incredulous.

"I didn't have any other place to go," he said, "except jump out of the belfry." Luckily, the nuns came to his rescue. "The nuns put a great priority on defending their modesty," he said.

And the parish priest insisted that Japanese *not* go upstairs out of respect for the nuns' piety. "Although the Japs thought they ought to check that belfry," said Vanderpool, "they didn't want to get in trouble by being accused of molesting nuns."

Reluctantly, the Japanese officer said: "All right, never mind."

Both companies left later that night.

A bit shaken from their latest close encounter, Vanderpool's team quickly departed the Catholic parish, and stealthily made their way to the eastern edge of Laguna de Bay. Upon reaching the shoreline, they wrangled a handful of canoes, and paddled westward across the gigantic lake. The darkness of the pre-dawn hours offered them *some* concealment, but time and distance were not on their side. Laguna de Bay was nearly 25 miles wide, and the Japanese patrolled it heavily at night—with high-luminescent searchlights affixed to the bows of their patrol boats. "We were a little bit edgy," he admitted. "We saw them, heard them, and we heard other boats being hailed. Fortunately for us, we weren't stopped."

Shortly before daybreak, Vanderpool and his canoe teams arrived on the western side of Laguna de Bay, the lakefront shores of Manila proper. Unloading their gear, Major Lazo ushered them into a small cluster of safe houses, where they could plan their next movements. "We were trying to figure out how to get across the next stretch," he said. Studying his map, Vanderpool deduced that they were at least ten miles from the nearest accessible waypoint. "We were on the southside of town," he recalled, "and if we could go about ten miles, we knew we had it made, because then we'd be in the rice paddy country where the Japs couldn't follow us in the dark, and we would be able to follow the native trails." This, in turn, would lead them to the nearest ROTC guerrilla outpost.

While contemplating their next move, Vanderpool asked himself: "What would you do if you were at home?" To which, he answered himself: "Hell, I'd call a taxi." Beaming, he turned to Major Lazo:

"Major Lazo, call a taxi."

"Call a taxi?!"

"Sure, call a taxi. If you want to go somewhere, you call a taxi if you don't have a car."

Lazo had never considered using a commercial taxi as a means of wartime transportation.

"I haven't either," said Jay, "let's try it."

Thus, Major Lazo called for a taxi—"and sure enough one came," said Vanderpool. "We could walk, of course, but that big old heavy radio, which worked worldwide, was a monster."

However, when the taxi driver realized his new fares were American commandos, he began to reconsider giving them a ride. Jay couldn't fault the driver for his apprehension—"because if he got caught, it would be his head, too." But when the cab driver made ready to flee, "We gave him the option that if he didn't do it, he was going to get hurt; but if he *did* do it, he'd be rewarded." To aid the reluctant cab driver into making a decision, Vanderpool quickly showed him a thick wad of cash—the "financial reward" he would receive in exchange for his compliance.

"And he became a very loyal Filipino," Jay emphasized.

"We only had to go about ten miles, so for that distance, he'd take a chance." Their ten-mile stretch across southern Manila was surprisingly uneventful. For as luck would have it, the cab driver had placed a Japanese flag on his radiator cap. "All Japanese soldiers had to salute the Japanese flag," said Vanderpool. Thus, whenever the cab passed through a Japanese checkpoint, "we'd get a big highball [salute] and breeze on through." Apparently, the local sentries thought that anyone behind the wheel of a car showcasing the flag of the Rising Sun was a loyal supporter of the Emperor's government. Thus, the Japanese guards waved the taxi through one checkpoint after another . . . completely unaware that the vehicle's occupants were American commandos.

Arriving at the southern edge of the city, Vanderpool and his gang dismounted the taxi, paying its flag-waving driver his lavish fare. As the now-wealthy cabbie disappeared back into the urban sprawl, Jay Vanderpool began the arduous trek into the lowland jungles and rice paddies of southern Luzon. "The rest of the night, we walked cross-country carrying that heavy gear," he recalled. "We didn't move very fast because of the loads we were carrying. We walked . . . to the west and south, until we ended up with the Hunters guerrillas on [Mount] Pico de Loro."

Mount Pico de Loro was a dormant volcano standing at 2,257 feet overlooking the southern coast of Manila Bay and Corregidor Island. The surrounding foothills provided dense jungles, perennial canopies, and terrain that favored defensive operations. In sum, the Pico de Loro vicinity was ideal for guerrilla and spy operations. "There, we set up camp, and I established my radio station and put it on the air, so we could let General Headquarters know we had gotten safely across."

Because MacArthur had given him such a broad mission directive, Vanderpool's opening communiques to General Headquarters outlined his intentions: he was embedding himself as a "liaison" to the ROTC guerrillas. These guerrillas, he said, had drawn their ranks from the best conventional units in the Philippines—including the PMA cadre and the Philippine Scouts. Their operational areas held the advantage of terrain, and they had an excellent redoubt over the capital city, Manila Bay, and Corregidor. By coordinating Allied operations with these guerrillas in southern Luzon, Vanderpool was certain that the US could facilitate recapturing Manila.

At the ROTC base camp, Vanderpool met Colonel Terry Adeveso and his command staff. "His staff was a well-trained, highly motivated group." Indeed, his G-2 and Inspector General were both Annapolis graduates; his Chief of Operations was a West Pointer; the G-1 (Chief of Personnel) had been a Secretary to the President of the Philippines; and his Chief of Logistics was a graduate of *Ecole de Guerre* in France. "So, he had a highly-professional group of people."

And Vanderpool was clear to explain his role as a "coordinator" and "facilitator."

He made no pretenses of having command authority over Colonel Adeveso or his guerrillas. "Terry had his own command, and I didn't try to run his command at all, but used his headquarters as a supporting system for my operations. As coordinator, I had no command responsibilities and also, as such, I had no unit responsibilities." His job was to increase the guerrillas' capacity to fight the Japanese, and facilitate joint operations with follow-on conventional forces when the time came. "So, one by one we met and visited . . . all the known guerrilla leaders in western Laguna, Cavite, and Batangas. Through them we established communications; those who didn't have radios we supplied, plus batteries and generators. We put out a very limited number of weapons and ammunition," with similarly small rations of medical supplies—"because we had so little." Still, Vanderpool and his team tried to distribute the supplies evenly.

"We started getting revenue returns when we started swapping pilots," he said, "that is, US Navy and Air Force pilots who had been shot down"—and subsequently recovered by Allied guerrillas. In fact, these downed aviators became a new form of "human currency," in exchange for military supplies, because "the Navy and Air Corps wanted their people back." Thus, the stage was set for Jay Vanderpool to bring these downed American pilots back to SWPA Headquarters en route to rejoining their home squadrons. Jay would bring the recovered pilots to a pre-selected rendezvous point along the shore, awaiting the next submarine, which in turn would ferry the pilots back to New Guinea or Australia. "We suggested that while they [the submarine crews] were picking pilots up, they could bring in a load of [various military supplies]. "So, they loaded a PBY [seaplane] or submarine with a bunch of goodies that we wanted, and we'd give them a couple of pilots. We never gave them all [the pilots] we had at one time; that would be killing the golden-egg goose. If we had three or four [pilots] we'd give them a couple."

In the midst of this pseudo-human trafficking scheme, Jay was nevertheless mindful to ensure the pilots' safety. For instance, he didn't bring all the recovered pilots to the central camp because: "that would be a risky concentration if we were overrun." He didn't want to risk all the pilots being killed if the ROTC base camp were suddenly attacked by the Japanese. "So, we'd leave them out at another camp." With every incoming submarine (and fresh delivery of supplies), Jay would hand off a few pilots, and then tell the submariners: "We have a couple pilots [farther inland]. Would you like to have them?"

Naturally, the crews wanted to bring back more pilots.

"So, we'd set up another rendezvous, and every time we gave them a few pilots, they gave us a load of supplies." All told, Jay Vanderpool and the Philippine guerrillas were quite happy with this trade agreement. "For example, we salvaged and traded 22 pilots in December 1944 alone.

Everyone was happy, and this became our limited resupply source. In fact, that was the main source of supplies we had until after the Americans landed in Luzon."

For their daily sustenance: "We didn't go hungry, but we didn't eat very well either," he said. "Our basic diet was rice, when we could get it. When we couldn't get rice, we ate corn . . . and sometimes rice mixed with horse corn." Admittedly, Vanderpool enjoyed eating rice—but having rice *every day* for breakfast, lunch, and dinner was enough to curb his enthusiasm for the dish. "Our breakfast rice could be sprinkled with brown sugar or grated coconut," he said. "Lunch rice was sometimes served with vegetable soup, when available. Dinner rice was sometimes improved with a little meat. Although there were many water buffaloes in the Philippines, they were so important to the farmer, he would not part with them at all. He would rather let you have two girl children than one carabao. Occasionally, some kind citizen would sell us a few chickens."

Meanwhile, American forces were fighting down in Leyte. From these developments, it was clear that the Allies were rolling back the tide of Japanese aggression, and a reconquest of the Philippines was imminent. Simultaneously, on the other side of the world, Allied forces had succeeded in securing a foothold in Italy, and had recently invaded Northern France. The combined American-British-ANZAC forces had been pushing the Germans back to the borders of the Fatherland. Despite a brief Axis counterattack in the

Ardennes (history would call it the "Battle of the Bulge"), the Allies were regaining the initiative and penetrating into the borders of the Reich.

With the Allies closing in on all fronts, Vanderpool re-emphasized to the guerrillas an important lesson he had learned during his pre-mission briefs in Hollandia: "Remember Warsaw." In other words: "Don't go jumping into taking on the Japanese Army by yourselves; because if you are wiped out you are no good to anyone. Wait until the Americans get here and then coordinate your work with that of the American ground forces, Air Force, or whatever it might be; but don't try to win the war by yourself, because you won't be any good to anyone." Understandably, it was a hard pill for many Filipinos to swallow. Their homeland had been invaded and they wanted to take it back *yesterday*.

Begrudgingly, however, they knew Vanderpool was right.

They knew they didn't have the resources to defeat the Japanese on their own.

"What we did in that period through November and December [1944] was coordinate and get communications established. We set up a pony express system throughout the entire area. At every barrio, we put up two or three ponies, so riders could come in and dismount every few miles; so we had a very effective pony express system." Of course, the small Philippine ponies weren't very fast—"They're not very good race horses," he said, "but they're better than a man trying to walk by himself."

Still, coordinating operations amongst the guerrillas was not without its growing pains. For example, some of the guerrilla units fought with each other more than they fought with the Japanese. Most of the in-fighting among the separate units were born of petty jealousies and unchecked egos. "They were after territorial power, ego power," said Jay. "And if they dominated a town; they were big wheels. If they were chased out of town, they'd go back and fight the guy that chased them out, even though he was another Filipino."

But the bigger problem was: "They were wasting ammunition."

Jay got into the middle of one such scuffle, telling the guerrillas to save their ammunition "and shoot the Japs with it." When Vanderpool explained it in those terms, "it sounded so logical that usually they wouldn't fight one another for three or four days afterwards."

Ego-driven power struggles notwithstanding, Jay's biggest concern was the ever-changing list of Japanese sympathizers. These spies, saboteurs, and puppet leaders were the unholy trinity of collaborators working against the Allied guerrilla movement. One of the more prominent Vichy-ite collaborators was Governor Castaneda, the Japanese puppet governor of the Cavite province. "He used his police power to harass some of the guerrilla leaders whom he considered as bandits or outlaws," said Jay. "He was at least partially right." Indeed, some real-life banditos had joined the ranks of local guerrilla units, using the pretext of war as a convenient way to eliminate their personal enemies, and justifying the homicides by claiming the target had been a "collaborator." As Vanderpool conceded: "Many guerrillas did more harm to Filipinos than to the Japanese." Still, many of the Southern Luzon guerrillas (whether patriots or outlaws) considered Castaneda a traitor for accepting the Japanese assignment.

Not keen to tolerating the caprices of a Vichy-ite governor, Jay decided to have a little talk with Castaneda himself—"against the advice of many guerrilla leaders." Still, Vanderpool was confident he could persuade the puppet leader to abandon his enemy ties. "I told him what he had done up to now was between himself and the new

Filipino post-war government. I further explained that whatever he did in the next few months would be between him and the United States government, and that any allegations of pro-Japanese actions could result in very adverse reports to General MacArthur." Castaneda also had to bear in mind that the Allies had already landed on Leyte, and were knocking on Japan's backdoor.

"He promised to help the Allied cause," said Vanderpool.

"He so promised, although he still thought most of the guerrillas were really bandits." Still, Vanderpool's talk had been enough to warrant Castaneda's reconsideration of his ties to the Japanese. If Castaneda could be prodded into helping the USAFFE guerrillas (even if by coercion) he could be useful in assisting the Allied war effort. "He had a large local following," said Jay, "and over 20 years military training we might be able to use."

During the meeting with Vanderpool, Castaneda was particularly critical of "General" Patricio Erni, claiming that he was the most dangerous bandit in the Cavite province, and the biggest menace to its people. Patricio Erni was one of the more notorious guerrilla leaders in southern Luzon. On paper, Erni was a *colonel*; but after the Fall of the Philippines, he proclaimed himself a general, claiming that he was commanding a corps-sized unit. In reality, however, this "corps" was no larger than a standard infantry brigade. "He had some cavalry, more nearly dragoons as they dismounted to fight," said Vanderpool. "His people dominated a large sector of Cavite. All of Erni's men were ready to fight anyone at any time. Quentin Gellidon [a Philippine Army colonel], who was one of my trusted advisors, knew Erni well and actually belonged to his organization."

Thus, with Gellidon in tow, Vanderpool set out to visit Erni.

Buoyed by his success in persuading Castaneda to support the Allied cause, Vanderpool surmised he could do the same with Erni, and channel their collective energy into fighting the Japanese instead of each other. "Knowing the respect Filipinos held for the .45 caliber pistol," said Jay, "I wore two .45s in cutaway tied-down holsters"—sporting a look reminiscent of the old Hollywood Westerns.

"I refused to take off my guns to meet the 'General,'" he continued.

And to Jay's surprise, he and General Erni got along quite well.

"I explained US policy, offered to help him with radios, medicine, ammunition, and a chance to shoot a lot of Japs later when the Americans landed in our sector. I also explained I had told Casteneda to stop wasting valuable ammunition shooting at Erni's men, and asked him to do the same."

Erni happily agreed.

"A lot of the other guerrillas thought he was pretty mean," Jay later recalled, "and he probably was. But Erni had a real fighting outfit. He had several battalions of battle-hardened troops, of whom I think quite a few he got from springing prisons."

Vanderpool made similar sales pitches to other local guerrilla leaders beyond the Hunters ROTC territory. He emphasized that the Americans were here to help, but "just don't go wasting our ammunition shooting Filipinos. Keep it. And when the time came, we'd all get together and shoot Japs to our hearts' content."

In the meantime, however, Vanderpool continued to make ready for the pending Allied invasion of Luzon. "This went along, as I say, in the fall of 1944." By New Year's 1945, he was elated to report that "we had established pretty good communication between the groups." Moreover, he had curbed the "unnecessary territorial bickering," among the local guerrilla factions. "We *reduced* the bickering," he emphasized, "we didn't stop it."

And then there was another group that caught his attention: the Hukbalahaps. "These communist troops were anti-Japanese, of course, and my theory was that they might be our enemy after this war, but at that time we were fighting the same enemy." As such, Vanderpool contacted the Huk leadership, informing them that he would provide them with ammunition and medical supplies, but no firearms. "They wanted more," Jay recalled, "but they thought that was better than nothing, so they accepted that."

As it turned out, Jay's hunch about the post-war Hukbalahap had been correct. After defeating their common enemy in the Japanese, the Huk initiated a full-scale insurgency against the post-war Philippine government, which carried on into the 1950s.

"So, we got ourselves ready for the American return," he continued. "I think it was probably in December [1944], I got a message from General Headquarters one day to come down to Leyte for a conference. I made an arrangement that if I could get down to Mindoro, where Commander [George] Rowe had a camp, he could bring in a PBY [seaplane] or a PT boat," thus facilitating Vanderpool's voyage to Leyte. Rowe was a US naval officer who operated a radar station on Mindoro.

Using a commandeered sailboat from the fishing club on Corregidor, Jay loaded a platoon of riflemen and some supplies for the trip into Mindoro. "We didn't have enough rice to stock the boat," he said. "All we had were some camotes, tasteless hard sweet potatoes. You can't eat them after they're cooked. We threw in a couple bushels for a one or two-day run and headed out to sea." Before setting sail, Vanderpool conferred with the two meteorologists whom he had brought with him during the voyage aboard the USS *Cero*.

"The weather looked pretty good to us," said Jay.

There were no identifiable low-pressure systems, or any data to give cause for concern.

"So, we got in the boat and set sail as soon as it got dark."

That's when a typhoon came through.

Indeed, the same typhoon that had pummeled the Allied landings in Leyte Gulf, was now making its way towards Vanderpool's sailboat. "About two o'clock in the morning this thing hit." Not being well-versed in sailboat operations, Jay scrambled to keep the boat steady as it took the full force of the typhoon's wind and waves.

He quickly dropped all the canvas, and brought the mast to "bare poles," as he called them. He then cried out to Major Lazo:

"Lazo, throw out a sea anchor!"

"What's a sea anchor?!" Lazo had no idea.

"Hell, I don't know," Jay thundered, "just throw one out anyway."

The pair scrambled below deck where they found an old mast down, "and we tied a bunch of junk to it, and then an old Manila line to that," before tossing their improvised "anchor" over the side.

Although the sailboat was now (hopefully) anchored in place, Vanderpool had to hope that his vessel could withstand the force of the typhoon. He didn't know how fast the winds were, "but I know the seas must have been 35 to 50 feet high, with a lot of spray on top. When we were down in the troughs, it wasn't too bad. But when you came to the top, boy it was windy up there."

To make matters worse, Jay didn't know how to navigate a ship at sea beyond using a simple magnetic compass. "I am at sea in a typhoon," he said, "and not a native sailor aboard, and the only navigational instrument was a little K&E compass I used to carry around my neck on a patrol. I could lay it parallel to a crack in the deck and navigate more or less." Still, there was little he could do until the storm passed.

"Everyone down below was of course, seasick."

The storm subsided sometime after nightfall. "We slept about an hour until sun-up," he said, "and we were out in the Pacific Ocean. We didn't have the slightest idea where we were; we could have been anywhere."

Maintaining his composure, Jay looked at his compass. "Well, we know this: if we keep going east, we'll hit something, some friendly land. If we go west, we'll end up in China or someplace." Finally, he vectored the sailboat due east, and soon came within sight of Lubang island.

Seeing Lubang was both a blessing and a curse.

On the one hand, Lubang was only a few miles from Mindoro—thus, Jay knew they hadn't drifted too far; they were still very much within the Philippine archipelago. On the other hand, the Japanese still had an active airfield on Lubang, an airbase that ran regular patrols along the surrounding sea lanes. "I didn't like it, but we couldn't do much about it. We got our sails up and started chugging along like crippled fishermen."

Almost on cue, the Japanese sent up a scout plane—"which came around and blinked his blinker,"—trying to assess whether this wayward sailboat was friendly or enemy. "We didn't have a blinker," said Jay, nor did he know the response pattern needed to indicate that the sailboat was "friendly." Thus, he stayed below deck, while a few of his Filipino guerrillas nonchalantly stood on the bow, smiling and waving friendly at the Japanese aircraft. They hoped that, so long as they waved at the passing pilot, he would take them for civilian mariners, and leave them unmolested.

"Finally, the Japanese waved back and flew away, for which we were quite happy."

Of greater relief, however, was that Vanderpool and his crew knew where they were. Maintaining their easterly course, Jay pulled out the only map in his possession—"a cutout from a *National Geographic* magazine which was only about eight by ten inches." Considering his own lack of seamanship, he knew that the best he could do was use his magnetic compass and hope for the best. "So, we just kept bearing east and, lo and behold, before sundown, a breeze came in"—giving them a good push to a speed of six knots. And, in just a few hours, the dark silhouette of Mindoro appeared just over the horizon.

"I'll be damned," said Jay.

His navigation via the handheld compass and *NatGeo* magazine map had put them on a course to the coastal city of Abra de Illog in Mindoro. "That's where Commander George Rowe had his camp. We put [the sailboat] right square in the middle of that channel. In the meantime, Rowe had sent some bancas out to meet us when he saw us coming in."

Wading to the beach of Rowe's camp, Vanderpool got on the radio and learned that an American landing force had just pulled into southern Mindoro at San Jose, where they had captured the local airfield. Thus, the Navy agreed to send up a section of PT boats to take Vanderpool to San Jose, whereupon he could board a C-47 to fly into Leyte. After being tossed about by a raging typhoon, Jay Vanderpool wasn't too keen on the idea of boarding another boat this soon. But, as he admitted, riding aboard the PTs was "fine travelling" compared to the storm-ridden sailboat. The PT crews also had food and hot coffee onboard.

Colonel Jay D. Vanderpool, circa 1958. Vanderpool bears the latter-day insignia of the Artillery Branch. Before the Air Defense Artillery separated into its own branch, all artillery officers wore the designated crossed cannons with the centered missile from 1957 until 1968.

Jay Vanderpool's hometown of Wetumka, Oklahoma.

A Civilian Conservation Corps (CCC) camp in Oklahoma, similar to the one Vanderpool joined in the mid-1930s. In the midst of the Great Depression, the CCC was one of many work-relief programs available for near-destitute young men like Jay Vanderpool.

Schofield Barracks, Hawaii, 1930s. Having grown restless as an itinerant young worker, Jay Vanderpool enlisted in the US Army in 1936. As a young artilleryman, his first duty assignment was in the Hawaiian Territory.

December 7, 1941. Wheeler Army Airfield goes up in flames under the fury of the Japanese attack. Vanderpool witnessed the devastation of Wheeler Field and Battleship Row that morning. By that evening, he was among a handful of survivors digging trenches along the beaches of Oahu, anticipating a Japanese invasion of the Hawaiian Islands.

USS *Cero*. The Submarine that ferried Vanderpool and his team of Allied liaisons into the Philippines

Major Jay Vanderpool (right) reviews the operational details for an upcoming mission, 1944.

Lieutenant Colonel Jay Vanderpool (center) confers with Brigadier General Everett E. Brown in Cagayan, Luzon (Philippines) showing him a sample leaflet order to be dropped on a sealed concentration of Japanese troops. June 28, 1945.

Vanderpool (left) confers with the 11th Airborne Division staff over some more leaflets to be dropped over North Luzon (Philippines) encouraging the Japanese to surrender.

An aerial photo of the Los Baños Prison Camp, one of the more notorious Japanese POW camps in the Philippine Islands.

Los Baños Prison Camp as seen from an Allied photo, with intel markings and labels to facilitate the camp's raid and liberation.

Filipino guerrillas turn over Japanese prisoners to the 25th Infantry Division. After the Fall of Bataan in 1942, various guerrilla factions populated the Philippine countryside, harassing the Japanese occupation force, and later fighting alongside conventional Allied forces during the reconquest of the Philippine Islands.

GHQ of the US Occupation Force in Japan, 1947. Following the Japanese surrender, Vanderpool served a number of years in Occupied Japan, overseeing the demilitarization of the Imperial Japanese forces.

An ROK guerrilla instructor teaches basic demolition skills to the other members of his unit. Throughout the Korean War, the UN made extensive use of indigenous partisan forces to conduct special operations. Jay Vanderpool would later command these UN partisans (whose ranks included North Korean and Red Chinese defectors) during the final years of the Korean Conflict.

Korean guerrillas receive communications training with the AN/GRC-9 radio set, circa 1952.

Fort Rucker, 1957. WO1 James Reagan poses in front of his experimental "Sky Cav" helicopter. Reagan was one among the infamous "Vanderpool's Fools"—men trying to adapt the helicopter into a close air support weapon.

Fort Rucker, 1957. Captain Charlie Jones, another alumnus of "Vanderpool's Fools."

"Vanderpool's Fools," including the pilots and maintenance crews, pose for a group photo, 1957.

The earliest helicopters in Vanderpool's test group, such as this Bell H-13, were one-man machines that seemed to pose more danger to the pilot than to any ground targets.

The full "Sky Cav" platoon prepares for another demonstration. To gain traction for the airmobile concept, Vanderpool's demonstration team toured various Army posts, performing maneuvers for anyone who would provide a captive audience.

The intrepid pilots of the early H-13 test helicopters.

Vanderpool and his men in the machine shop at Fort Rucker.

The first airmobile test platoon,
delivering soldiers to the field via helicopter.

Fort Rucker, 1956. The original Air Cavalry Test Team (aka "Vanderpool's Fools"). Pictured from left to right are: (standing) Captain Harold Henning; Colonel Jay Vanderpool; Captain James "Monty" Montgomery; (seated) Sergeant Quinn and Specialist Whittner.

Spring 1958. Sporting his Army summer uniform with regulation shorts and knee-high socks, Jay Vanderpool (second from right) speaks with a visiting delegation at Fort Rucker.

Spring 1958. Jay Vanderpool (far left) reviews Air Cavalry project requirements with representatives from other Army branches. Stressing the need for synergy in combat, Air Cavalry had to reconcile its mission parameters against the limitations and capabilities of its sister branches – including the infantry, artillery, and logistics.

Jay Vanderpool thanks Bob Hope for his Christmas Show in Vietnam. December 26, 1966.

The experimental Bell UH-1 "Huey" helicopter, which would become the mainstay of American airmobile forces in Vietnam. The prototype Huey was one of among several that Jay Vanderpool tested and evaluated during the course of his duties in building airmobile warfare.

A prototype Bell attack helicopter. These choppers would become the proverbial "big guns" of the Air Cavalry until the arrival of the AH-64 Apache helicopter, years later. Both platforms, however, can trace their lineage to Vanderpool's diligence in adapting close air support armaments to rotary-wing aircraft.

Fort Rucker, 1977. With his wife, Lynn, present,
Jay D. Vanderpool is inducted into the Aviation Hall of Fame.

However, their voyage along the Mindoro Strait down into San Jose was no pleasure cruise. "On the way down," said Vanderpool, "a Japanese patrol plane spotted us. He came in and made the usual circle, blinked his signal light, so we signaled our reply for the day. It apparently didn't check out correctly. He swung around to the rear to set up his bombing run."

The PT boats went into survival mode.

As the Japanese pilot closed in to about 300 feet, "the skippers held their course at full throttle until bombs away. At that time, they split the PTs [formation] apart about 20 degrees each; one left, one right, and all guns opened up. As the plane went between us with his stick of bombs, the machine gunners got him." The Japanese pilot splashed into the horizon about one-half mile ahead.

Jay Vanderpool arrived at the San Jose airfield no worse for wear, but the Japanese weren't done yet. Within minutes of his arrival, a flight of Mitsubishi G4M "Betty" bombers appeared overhead. Scrambling for cover, Jay was disappointed that "the best cover I could find was an empty swimming pool, which is bigger than the foxhole you really want." And these Betty bombers were delivering something he had never seen before—a parachute bomb. Several yards away, Vanderpool spied a fellow soldier firing his rifle at one of the parachute bombs. Jay thought to himself: "Well, he's a pretty good shot, but not very good on judgement." Indeed, the fellow soldier kept firing at the bomb from an unsafe distance while it floated to the ground. "He finally got it when it was about 100 feet over his head," said Jay.

"That was the end of that soldier."

Jay, meanwhile, had been protected from the blast by taking cover in the empty swimming pool. "Anyway, we got through that," he continued. "The Air Corps loaned me an airplane, an old

C-47 gooney bird, that drove me over to Tacloban, Leyte . . . to go to this briefing at General Headquarters."

The SWPA Headquarters briefing went on for several days, and featured every key player of the Allied war effort. "A number of the commanders and senior staff officers were planning for the final offensive in the central and northern Philippines," said Jay. "Every operation was outlined in detail." There would be a number of amphibious landings on Luzon, and plans to dig the Japanese out of the Cordillera Central. The plans were solid, well-conceived, and well-articulated. But, as Vanderpool noted, receiving this level of information was also a liability. "Once you had that information," he said, "you were supposed to go on a 'No Capture' list . . . you were not to be taken alive." Essentially, if one were about to be captured, he could either fight to the death or save the last bullet for himself.

At one point during the briefing, HQ yielded the floor to Vanderpool, allowing him to give his report on the enemy situation in his sector of Luzon. Although he had been operating autonomously as a liaison to the Allied guerrillas, he still belonged to the G-2 Intelligence Staff of SWPA, and his reports were channeled through that staff section. As Vanderpool began his portion of the brief, however, the G-2 asked him to confirm reports of an alleged Japanese division defending the beach at Nusugbu—a municipality just south of Cavite province.

Jay was befuddled.

There was no such "division" at Nusugbu.

To the contrary, Jay informed them that this enemy contingent at Nusugbu was nothing more than: "a rifle company, minus one platoon, plus two extra machine guns. That's it—period."

Vanderpool's disclosure sent the General Staff into a frenzy.

"This had everyone upset," he recalled. "The G-3 [Operations] asked how old this information was." Vanderpool replied that the intel was five days old at most.

"How do you know?" the G-3 demanded.

"I had been down there buying sugar," Jay replied.

He had also spoken to the mayor about it.

Vexed by their own intelligence blunder, some of the senior staff wanted to know what had happened to the estimated "division" which they were certain had landed in the vicinity.

"What happened to their tanks?" they asked.

Jay replied that the main body of the Japanese task force had gone north of Manila. He had been keeping close tabs on the intra-guerrilla comms network, and could verify that the highest concentration of enemy troops were populating in North and Central Luzon. "Anyway, some people believed it and some didn't."

Nevertheless, HQ decided to send a reconnaissance team into Nusugbu to verify Vanderpool's claim. "If I was right, the landing force would push north. If the old intelligence [i.e., the G-2's original assessment regarding the Japanese division] was right, we would at least have another beachhead on Luzon. Of course, history later proved I was right."

By this point during the briefing, Jay was growing tired of listening to the endless carousel of field-grade and flag-rank officers argue over petty details of the various landings. Amidst the confusion, Vanderpool quietly snuck out of the meeting. "Probably I shouldn't have done it," he later reflected, but he wanted to get back to his team on Luzon.

The G-3 staff had already secured a Navy PBY seaplane to fly Vanderpool back to Mindoro—"and I went down and snuck out that night. I flew back the next morning and landed in the river at

Abra de Illog, Mindoro, again where I'd been before." He borrowed another canoe from Commander Rowe's intel team, which he paddled over to Looc Cove on Luzon. "From there, I walked up the hill, got on my radio, and reported myself back in position. There wasn't much they could do about it then. I was already back, and they couldn't tell me to go back [to Leyte], because I was already there [in Luzon]."

Vanderpool later found out that General Willoughby had considered recalling him to the G-2 section permanently—essentially stripping Jay of the "liaison" role and putting him to work in the staff headquarters. Willoughby didn't care that Vanderpool had left the briefing early; rather, he thought Vanderpool knew too much, and therefore was too much of a liability if captured.

Fortunately, General Willoughby let him stay in the liaison role. Nevertheless, Vanderpool understood the G-2's concern.

"You see, I knew where all the landings were going to be, and on what dates. Really, you shouldn't be wandering around behind enemy lines with that information in your head. However, I hated to quit when it was that late, and I figured if the Japs got me, I wouldn't last long enough to talk anyway. I wasn't too worried because the Japs were already very unhappy with me."

As it turned out, Vanderpool had been on the Japanese's "all-star" hit list for quite some time. In fact, the Japanese were convinced that Vanderpool was a Major General. But the misattributed rank was, as he called it, "a comedy of errors." The Japanese had earlier intercepted some of Vanderpool's written correspondence. He signed every letter with the salutation: "Jay D. Vanderpool, Major, General Staff Corps." When the Japanese translated his intercepted communiques, they put "Major" and "General" together, assuming him to be a two-star general. "Some people accused me of doing this deliberately," he later recalled, "but I didn't." And because the Japanese thought Vanderpool to be a high-ranking flag officer, they subsequently assumed that the guerrilla forces were much larger than their true size.

"Anyway, I got back up there [on Luzon] and we started doing our final broad planning." The final reconquest of the Philippines was close at hand, yet Jay had to keep the invasion details to himself. "I couldn't tell the guerrillas anything," he said, "because it was bad enough for me to have it in my head without having that information in other people's heads." Even at this late stage in the war, operational plans were on a need-to-know basis. "I didn't tell them anything, and I know they were curious, but they were too polite to say so, too well-trained to say so."

A few days later, on January 9, 1945, the Operation MIKE-I task force hit the beaches of Lingayen Gulf, securing the Allies' toehold on North Luzon. That morning at breakfast, Vanderpool announced to the Hunters ROTC that the Americans had just landed in Lingayen Gulf. "The guerrillas looked at me," he said, "and you could just see the disbelief." Considering the tight-lipped discretion that he had displayed since returning from Leyte, the guerrillas were reluctant to believe him. Their suspicion turned to joy, however, when the news broadcasts confirmed that the Americans had, in fact, made landfall at Lingayen Gulf.

A few days later, Allied forces were in Manila.

But now that the Americans had arrived, the Japanese grew more desperate to keep Luzon under Axis control. In late January, the Manila garrisons began pouring into the countryside, determined to crush the faceless spies and guerrillas who were feeding intelligence to Allied forces.

Jay Vanderpool had a close call with one of these grudge patrols on the night of January 28. His team had just gone to sleep for the night, but his intuition kept gnawing at him. For some reason, his so-called "spider senses" were telling him that he had been at his current location (a camp in the foothills of Pico de Loro) for too long. "Let's get out of this place," he told himself, "It's hot."—i.e., 'hot' referring to a situation where enemy forces may be close at hand. Jostling his team awake, he told them:

"OK, we're going to move to our alternate location."

His team was not impressed.

"There was a lot of grumbling, of course, people were tired and about ready to go to sleep. Yet, they got up, and we struck camp. We decided to leave the fires burning. We left the fires burning, went down that little canyon, up across the other side to [a ridgeline with] an alternate [campsite] we had, carrying all that heavy gear through the woods."

His intuitive hunch, however, had been prophetically correct.

Shortly after midnight, the Japanese attacked the former campsite.

"All hell broke loose where we had been," said Vanderpool. "The Japs *did* attack that night, with machine guns, mortars, rifle platoons, but we were safely on the other ridge."

How fortunate that Vanderpool had listened to his gut.

The next morning, Vanderpool and his men awoke to the sound of naval gunfire. American battleships were pounding the beaches at Nasugbu—a preparatory bombardment for the Operation MIKE-VI landing force. "That's when the 11th Airborne Division came over the beach for their landing in the south," Jay recalled. When the 11th Airborne's advance reconnaissance scouts arrived in South Luzon, the guerrillas ushered them into Vanderpool's command post. For the scouts, he outlined every bit of information he had available: troop dispositions, firepower capabilities, supply nodes, and routes of egress and ingress.

"There was still a very light Japanese force in there [Nasugbu]," he added—the same company-sized element he had referred to during the Headquarters briefing on Leyte. Naturally, the 11th Airborne's frontline regiments made short work of the company-sized Japanese defenders, and started up the highway towards Manila.

"At that time," said Jay, "I had deployed most of the guerrillas along the MSR, the main supply route [leading into Manila proper]. I guess 90 percent of them were on that mission, so when the 11th Airborne hit Manila, their beachhead was about 50 feet wide and 50 miles deep, because the guerrillas secured the flanks all the way up, on the main thrust, going north."

When the Division Staff landed on Luzon, Vanderpool reported to Major General Joseph Swing, the 11th Airborne Division commander. To assist the Division in its drive into Central and North Luzon, General Swing gave Vanderpool the mission of "gathering, coordinating, and organizing all the guerrillas in the Southern Provinces."

But by now, Jay Vanderpool had already done more than half of the legwork.

The guerrillas were ready; they just needed a mission.

And, over the ensuing months, his guerrillas would execute a series of supporting attacks, flank security missions, recon patrols, and spy jobs.

During the guerrillas' first major operation with the 11th Airborne Division, Jay recalled that: "we hit the Japs just south of Manila, before we had any real resistance." There was, however, a Japanese division on their eastern flank, but as Vanderpool noted:

"They didn't leave the hills at all. They just stayed there." That Japanese division must have been under orders to hold their position, because "they didn't bother us much."

While the 11th Airborne met its fierce resistance south of Manila, Vanderpool's guerrillas were protecting the division's right flank—covering what would have been a sizeable gap between their right flank and the shores of Laguna de Bay. "It must have been a couple thousand yards," he estimated. For the occasion, Vanderpool rounded up eleven of his best guerrilla companies and put them abreast. "I knew the Japs were dug in with a reinforced battalion up on a couple little hills, near Sagumbayan. I had a lot of rifle ammunition that day, but I didn't have machine guns, nor artillery, so I decided to use marching fire." In other words, the guerrillas would lay down suppressive fire using their rifles while literally *walking* towards the enemy objective. Under these auspices, the guerrillas would fire their weapons without stopping to aim, using their mobile volume of fire to pin down the Japanese before engaging them in close combat.

"I had an ammunition truck coming up to top-off [our ammunition] that night," he recalled. "We deployed the force in a peculiar order of battle."

In fact, the guerrillas themselves were a peculiar (and a surprisingly diverse) bunch.

"We had some Filipino battalions," he said, "then we also had a battalion of Chinese Nationalists, and a battalion of Chinese Communists." As incredulous as it may have sounded, the Kuomintang and Red Chinese both had guerrilla operations in the Philippines. The Maoist guerrillas had drawn their ranks from the Filipinos of Chinese descent, of whom there were many in Luzon. These Maoists fought under the banner of the *Wha-Chi* guerrilla organization—also known as the "Chinese-Filipino Anti-Japanese Guerrilla Forces." The Chiang Kai-shek guerrillas, on the other hand, had mobilized a high number of Kuomintang loyalists from among the Chinese Filipinos. Even the Hukbalahap sent a battalion to aid Vanderpool in his efforts. The Huks' arrival was a godsend, as it allowed Vanderpool to put a buffer between the Red and Nationalist Chinese. "In between those two," said Jay, "I put the Filipino Hukbalahap Communists to keep the Chinese from fighting one another, and to keep the other Filipinos from fighting the Huks."

The marching fire operation turned out beautifully. This motley crew of Red Chinese, Kuomintang, Huk, and Philippine Army/ROTC guerrillas stormed the Japanese hilltops at Bagumbayan with minimal Allied casualties. When describing the mechanics of marching fire, Vanderpool said: "You put your rifle on your right hip, hold it with both hands, every time your left foot hits the ground you pull the trigger. Everyone fires straight to the front, not aiming at anything, just firing straight ahead. And it's amazing the amount of random fire you can put on an area with marching fire. We used a lot of ammunition routing the Japs." So much ammunition, in fact, that Vanderpool earned a mild reprimand from the Division staff.

But, in Vanderpool's eyes, it was better to use too much than too little.

And they couldn't argue with his results.

"A few days later a regiment from the 24th Infantry Division came in and replaced my men on these little hills I had taken."

After their relief-in-place, Jay and the guerrillas "pulled back and went into a bivouac for the night." They had been fighting the Japanese in continuous combat for the past ten days; and, understandably, they were exhausted. Setting up their bivouac,

Vanderpool's men settled themselves in a barrio of Nipa huts (traditional Philippine thatched houses built on stilts). "I had 11 reinforced companies in the houses on either side of the road," he recalled. But the guerrillas and the 24th Infantry Division troops were apparently so tired, that even the nightwatchmen fell asleep. Indeed, nearly every American or Filipino sentry in Vanderpool's sector fell asleep on duty that night.

This allowed an entire Japanese rifle battalion to walk through the Allied sector undetected.

"They walked through the American regiment," he recalled, "and then came down this road. Our first three outposts didn't see them either." They had all fallen asleep. The Japanese, meanwhile, continued their march unmolested, and completely unaware that they had wandered into an Allied sector. Finally, about a half-mile down the road, one of Vanderpool's semi-lucid sentries noticed the strange figures stomping around in the dark. That sentry challenged the forward elements of the Japanese column, all of whom were marching along with their rifles slung.

Seconds later, the guerrillas opened fire.

The other guerrillas, now jostled from their sleep, leapt out of their Nipa huts, and joined in the fusillade of the hasty ambush. Vanderpool remarked that it was the most beautifully-executed impromptu ambush he had ever seen. As Vanderpool described it, the Japanese had walked right into a shooting gallery—"our guerrillas fell on top of them, and started chewing them up."

Vanderpool was pleased that the hasty ambush had played out so well. But he was none too happy that his sentries (and those from the 24th Infantry Division), had let the Japanese column slip through their checkpoints. Then, too, Jay understood that his guerrillas and fellow soldiers were nearing the point of exhaustion. "It was the first time they had a chance to sleep," he said, "so they went to sleep, including our guards. The 24th Division's guards, I might say, didn't notice them going by either, so I don't care if it goes into the record."

But by every measure, "it was a hell of a firefight," said Jay. The first shots rang out at about four o' clock in the morning. By daybreak, the guerrillas were cutting down survivors with their bolo knives.

"I couldn't believe it," he said.

Aside from the depth charges they had dropped into the canyon on Guadalcanal, Jay had never seen a bloodier mess. These Filipino guerrillas had annihilated more than 90% of a Japanese battalion, at a loss of only 18–20 friendly KIAs. As Vanderpool recalled, the enemy dead "were lying all over the place. The guerrillas piled them in windrows along the road"—stacking them several feet high—"for the burial parties to handle later."

Word of the bloody ambush spread quickly. Within hours, Vanderpool received a call from Colonel Doug Quandt, the 11th Airborne Division's Chief of Staff.

"What in the hell is going on over there?" Quandt bellowed.

"Oh, we just had a firefight over here with a regiment of Japs," said Vanderpool, nonchalantly.

"So, we killed them."

Quandt was not amused.

"Boy, after all that ammunition you wasted the day before yesterday, General Swing is going to eat your head off."

But Jay Vanderpool, not one to suffer fools gladly, fired back:

"Why don't you ask him to come over and take a look at it?"

Quandt accepted the challenge and brought General Swing along with a slew of other officers to inspect the damage. "They came over in Jeeps," said Vanderpool, "and when they looked at those bodies stacked up for almost half a mile, a couple of them got sick. General Swing then turned to his aide and said:

"Give Vanderpool all the goddamn ammunition he wants."

Following the bloody ambush, Jay's guerrillas were tasked to feed the incoming refugees from Manila. He looked forward to tackling a humanitarian mission, and SWPA gave him a sum of money to buy rice, chickens, and pigs to feed the tens of thousands of refugees being process by Allied forces. Jay succeeded in nourishing *some* of the tagged refugees, but admitted that the guerrillas didn't have the resources to render civil aid to the Red Cross level. It was during the midst of this humanitarian relief when the Allied Command began discussing the liberation of the Los Baños Prison Camp. "Los Baños was an internment camp near the south end of Laguna de Bay, where the Japs were holding a thousand or so civilian internees, including a large percentage of women and some children, all suffering from starvation and sundry prison-type diseases."

Jay wasn't sure what triggered the sudden interest in Los Baños, but he surmised it was prompted by the Allies' arrival in and around Manila. The Sixth US Army under General Walter Kruger had landed north at Lingayen Gulf, and liberated the POW camp at Santo Tomas during the drive to Manila. "That liberation," said Vanderpool, "resulted in a lot of news media acclaim,

international attention and liberating heroes." It also brought to light the immense cruelty with which the Japanese were treating their prisoners, military and civilian. Thus began the sense of urgency to liberate as many camps as possible, especially those that were holding traditional non-combatants like women and children.

"General Robert Eichleberger, then commanding the Eighth US Army, was attacking Manila from the south and, along with a few staff officers, was forward at the headquarters of the 11th Airborne Division. General Eichelberger asked me if I could take guerrillas and liberate Los Baños."

Vanderpool wanted to say "yes," but he knew he didn't have the resources.

Moreover, his guerrillas were strangers to these isolated American prisoners.

"All we had were bancas," he recalled, "and those bancas are pretty rough for sick people, women, and kids to be getting in and out of, and particularly in the dark. Begrudgingly, Jay replied:

"No, I don't think we can do it."

"Well, I can get some amphibious tractors for you," said Eichelberger. "Can you do it with amphibious tractors?"

Vanderpool stood his ground.

"I don't want to go in with an all-guerrilla combat force," he replied. "We need the American flag on the ground, to talk those Americans in that camp into coming out. They're not going to believe a bunch of raggedy-tail guerrillas are safe to take them 40 or 50 miles through enemy territory. I'd be very hesitant to go if I was an internee."

Jay later recalled: "I did not accept the responsibility of pulling out 1,000–1,200 [or thereabouts] women and kids, and sick men, with my forces. If we got cut off out there, the Japs had a full infantry division right around the area. With an infantry division around us, they'd annihilate every person we had in the force."

Vanderpool was all for fighting the enemy.

But he didn't want to engage in a fight he couldn't win.

"I thought it would be foolhardy to take that risk when the campaign was so nearly over," he continued, "unless the Japanese started slaughtering the internees. If they started slaughtering the prisoners, yes we'd go, but until they start that final slaughter . . . I didn't want to do it. I think that General Eichelberger understood and agreed with me."

Jay reiterated his position to General Swing in the 11th Airborne, telling him: "If I go with the Americans, I would just act as a coordinator for the guerrillas on your flanks." Moreover, Jay wasn't a paratrooper. He had never been to jump school, and he had a very limited knowledge of parachutes.

"I don't know how to jump," said Vanderpool.

"Jump?!" Swing guffawed. "Hell, there's nothing to it. The sergeant kicks you out and the ground stops you. Sure you can jump."

Vanderpool and Swing both laughed.

Subsequently, the Allied leadership decided to liberate Los Baños by using the 11th Airborne Division as its main effort, "supported by guerrillas on the flanks in a neutralizing role." The Los Baños task force, as Vanderpool recalled, was to be reinforced by artillery, plus a combat engineer team to reinforce and maintain the bridges.

Vanderpool alerted his men to the mission, and the guerrillas assumed their security positions along the flanks of the US paratroopers. It was, as Jay re-emphasized, a "neutralizing role." In other words, they were to guard the division's flanks, and engage the enemy only if the flanking positions were threatened directly. The guerrillas did, however, send a number of scouts into the camp to locate "machine guns, guards, and things like that," Jay added.

"As you know, the 11th Airborne task force with Amtracks [amphibious tractors] went in and did a fine job, picked up the people, put them in the Amtracks and brought them back up to the western beach at Laguna de Bay." The Americans had just taken over an old municipal prison, where they boarded the refugees overnight. It seemed tragically ironic that these liberated civilian POWs were now being horded into *another* prison to receive proper medical attention. Still, the metro prison was a step up from the *ad hoc* prison camp at Los Baños.

"It was a good, dry place," said Jay.

But the interior dryness was where the new prison's merits ended. It was dry, yes, but it was also infested with fleas.

"We fed them. The doctors started segregating them for medical work, whatever was necessary to do."

As it turned out, facilitating the evacuation and intake of the Los Baños refugees marked the end of Jay Vanderpool's role as an SWPA liaison. "A few days after the Los Baños operation, we attached most of the guerrilla forces to American infantry regiments and artillery battalions. This had two purposes. One was American control when we were getting into some organized fighting; the second was to provide logistics for guerrillas who had no source of food or supplies." Now that the guerrillas were attached to American units full-time, Vanderpool's liaison work was effectively over. "I was then without any real job in the role as coordinator," he said, "so I got permission to leave and go back to rejoin my old division, the 25th Infantry Division, which was then up in northeastern Luzon, attacking towards Balete Pass, trying to open a hole into the Cagayan Valley where many remaining major Japanese military forces were concentrated." Upon Vanderpool's return to the Division, he was promoted to lieutenant colonel and given the job of Division G-2, which he kept until the occupation of Japan.

"We fought at Balete Pass for several weeks or months," said Jay, "and it was a very slow, head-knocking operation."

Indeed it was.

The Assistant Division Commander was killed by sniper fire.

"We were extracting the cost of about a dead Jap per yard of advance. We took moderate casualties"—685 American KIA versus 7,750 of the enemy. "We finally, by series of shallow double envelopments, took the road going through Balete Pass to the Cagayan Valley. After we took the pass, my division was pulled out," and placed in the rear.

In recognition for his service on Guadalcanal and in the Philippines, Jay Vanderpool was awarded the Silver Star Medal, Legion of Merit, and the Philippine Military Medal of Merit. He was also granted temporary R&R leave back to the United States. "It was my first trip back [to the US mainland] since 1937," he said, "for which I was quite happy."

But as Jay settled into his well-deserved R&R, the Imperial Japanese government refused to quit the fight.

5

After the Fire

Decompressing from the horrors of combat, Vanderpool spent much of his R&R catching up on events from the past four years. Indeed, by the time Jay returned to American soil, Germany had surrendered, the Führer was dead, and the Japanese were preparing to make their last stand in the Pacific. One by one, the enemy strongholds on Tarawa, Saipan, Iwo Jima, Okinawa and the Philippines collapsed under the power of Allied offensives.

With Germany out of the war, the US began sending more of its personnel to the Pacific. But even as the Allies closed in on the main archipelago, the Japanese refused to quit. Wanting to bring this destructive conflict to an end, and well aware of the bloodbath which would follow an invasion of the Japanese homeland, President Harry Truman made a profound, yet difficult decision: the atomic bomb would make its debut over the Empire of Japan.

Following the nuclear devastations of Hiroshima and Nagasaki, the Japanese government finally lost its will to fight. On August 14, 1945, Emperor Hirohito broadcasted a pre-recorded radio speech announcing his nation's unconditional surrender. He instructed all Imperial troops to lay down their arms and to cooperate with the newly arriving occupation force. Finally, on September 2, in a ceremony held aboard the USS *Missouri*, a Japanese delegation signed the official document of surrender.

With the stroke of a pen, the great World War II had finally come to an end.

Watching these events unfold from the States, Jay was glad that the war was finally over. It had been the greatest conflict in human history, drawing men from all walks of life into its service. He had begun the war as an entry-level Second Lieutenant. Now, four years later, he was a Lieutenant Colonel. But although the war had ended, his time in uniform was far from over. His rough-and-tumble upbringing had already given him an edge of maturity; and the war had matured him even further. As an artillery soldier, and now as an officer, he realized he had found his calling. Jay Vanderpool decided to stay in uniform.

"When I came back from the States, my division was getting ready to go to Japan," he recalled. "We had been preparing for the invasion of Japan." Under the original plan, the 25th Infantry Division was expected to hit the beaches of Honshu. But, as Jay admitted: "That would have been pretty rough, because I expected to get a regiment within a few days. We were figuring that the odds were we would need a new regimental commander in the division every other day." Indeed, prior to the Japanese surrender, civilians were digging trenches along the beach, and others were being issued pitchforks to attack incoming paratroopers.

That September, the 25th Division landed in Nagoya on the main island of Honshu.

Vanderpool wondered how the Japanese would greet him and his fellow GIs. He had seen first-hand the atrocities carried out by the Rising Sun. Given the savagery of their wartime conduct, many wondered if the Japanese truly intended to abide by their surrender, or if a few "dead-enders" would continue to fight against the Allied occupation.

Landing in Nagoya, however, Jay and his comrades discovered a hauntingly different picture: the Japanese *avoided* Americans at all costs. Some even refused to make eye contact. Others simply ran in the opposite direction if approached by a US serviceman. One soldier noticed that there were no women in sight. The few women who did sneak out into the daylight "had on baggy clothes to hide any female identification. Evidently, the Japs expected us to come in raping and looting as they always did."

Another soldier, WC Kitchen, remembered an incident where he was stopped by a Japanese officer and asked, "Why don't you rape and loot and burn? We would."

Kitchen just looked at the man in disbelief.

"That man was genuinely puzzled by our actions," he said. "I am ashamed to tell you what an inadequate reply I gave to that man. What an opportunity I had to tell him about our God and His laws, about our traditions . . . all we wanted was peace and respect and we would do the same for others, even our enemies. Well, I mumbled something about 'we just don't do things like that.' And that was the end of it."

The occupation itself, however, was a complex and multi-layered endeavor. Apart from the MPs, no one in the 25th Division had been trained for constabulary duty. Vanderpool and his men were now, in equal parts: policemen, peacekeepers, ambassadors, and first-responders. Of course, it would take time to deprogram four years of hostility, but the Japanese and Americans at least appeared committed to re-building peace.

One of the first priorities for the incoming occupation troops like Vanderpool was to ensure smooth operation of the Allied food distribution network. Following the collapse of the Imperial government, and the widespread destruction of most major cities, several million Japanese were now starving. Initially, the US government provided emergency food relief through the Government Aid & Relief in Occupied Areas (GARIOA) initiative. Throughout 1946, GARIOA spent more than $90 million to alleviate Japan's postwar hunger crisis.

And, just as Vanderpool had heard during his pre-war briefing from General Short in Hawaii, the US was committed to preserving the reign of Emperor Hirohito. Subsequently, the blame for Japan's wanton aggression throughout the Pacific, was placed at the feet of Prime Minister Hideki Tojo and the militarist government. Collectively, the Allies knew that if they wanted to secure Japan's postwar cooperation, the Emperor had to be kept beyond reproach.

Thus, General MacArthur set out to win Hirohito's support.

While other Allied leaders pushed for the Emperor to abdicate his throne and be charged as a war criminal, MacArthur stood fast in maintaining the Emperor's immunity, arguing that such a move would be wildly unpopular with the Japanese people.

When MacArthur and Hirohito met for the first time on September 27, 1945; the two stood together for a photograph that would become one of the most iconic images in Japanese history. The stark height difference between MacArthur (6'0") and Emperor Hirohito (5'5") left no question to the Japanese as to who was in charge now. With the full cooperation of Japan's monarchy, however, the Allied occupation now had a base of legitimacy with the Japanese population.

After staying a few weeks in Nagoya, the 25th Infantry Division occupied its new headquarters in Osaka, whereupon they assumed a wide swath of operational control over southwestern Honshu. "We had about 40 percent of industrial Japan in our sector," said Jay. "Our main job there was to make sure the Japanese were properly demilitarized and demobilized." On September 15, 1945, the Japanese Imperial Headquarters was dissolved; and, by December of that year, all Japanese military forces within the main archipelago had been disbanded. Throughout the occupation, Allied forces demolished (and dumped into the sea) more than two million tons of Japanese ammunition and equipment. "We undertook, with troops and a few civilians, to check the demilitarization," Jay recalled—specifically, the "conversion of industry from military to civil uses."

Reflecting on the former enemy's cooperation, Vanderpool noted: "The Japanese did a fine job on demobilizing." In fact, he was often surprised by the hospitality of the Japanese people. As their initial fears of the American occupation faded away, he found them to be very pleasant and sociable. It was a stark difference from the rabid fanaticism he had seen on the battlefields of Guadalcanal, New Georgia, and the Philippines. But now that the war had ended, Emperor Hirohito instructed them to be friendly and hospitable towards the Americans. And the Japanese happily obeyed their Emperor. In fact, by 1947, it seemed as though Vanderpool's occupation duty had become more of a goodwill tour.

Jay recalled that it was an interesting time to be in the Army. Many of the wartime volunteers and conscripts were being discharged, and the first round of replacement troops were arriving for occupation duty. By now, the Japanese no longer feared their American occupiers. However, the GIs—excited that the war was over and with little else to keep them busy—often ventured into town, got drunk, and engaged in colorful antics that the local Japanese didn't find amusing.

Between their mundane tasks of occupation duty, several GIs had taken to sampling the local varieties of Japanese beer . . . and the local variety of Japanese women. The Japanese had no societal hang-ups about sex—and the American GIs took full advantage of it. Several soldiers even kept Japanese girlfriends in the local towns. At first, American troops were forbidden to fraternize with Japanese civilians. But local commanders often looked the other way so long as the romantic liaisons didn't interfere with a soldiers' regular duties. Still, during that first year of the occupation, it wasn't unusual for the MPs to pick up a handful of GIs from a drunken caper, or for a soldier to miss his morning formation because he had overslept at a girlfriend's house.

The occupation duty did, however, bring some very unpleasant run-ins with the Japanese. One of the more unsavory aspects of Vanderpool's duty included processing the Japanese repatriates and POWs coming back into Honshu. As Japan's conquered territory returned to Allied control, the Imperial troops and Japanese colonists living in the outer Pacific were boarded onto ships and taken back to Japan. Stung by their defeat, and having lost everything in the war, these repatriated Japanese were timid, despondent, and sometimes combative with their American handlers. Nearly all of them were sick and many suffered from diseases they had gotten en route to the mainland. Throughout 1946, Allied forces repatriated more than five million Japanese back into the mainland.

Around this time, Jay also won the affections of a Miss Adelyn Mary "Lynn" Kozy, a Red Cross employee who was one year his senior. Occupied Japan was an unusual place to initiate a courtship, but theirs wasn't the only destination wedding on Japanese soil that year. Indeed, a number of US servicemen had taken their fiancées into Occupied Japan to exchange vows at various landmarks that had survived the Allied bombings. Jay and Lynn were married on February 4, 1947 at the Naku Ward Office in Yokohama, Japan. Their civil wedding was officiated by the US Vice Consul Otis W. Rhoades.

But as Jay and Lynn settled into their lives as newlyweds, his former colleagues in South Luzon were becoming targets of a political "witch hunt." During the war, several of the Allied guerrilla units had (out of necessity) executed enemy spies and collaborators.

When the families of these executed collaborators broke their silence, they lobbied the Philippine government to punish those responsible for the deaths of their loved ones. When the news reached General Eisenhower, who was now the Army Chief of Staff, he penned a letter to General MacArthur in Tokyo, saying that these latter-day justice warriors needed to be quashed. MacArthur in turn sent a communique to General James E. Moore, Commander of the Philippine Ryukyu Command. MacArthur tapped Russel Volckmann, the former leader of the North Luzon guerrillas, to lead the exoneration efforts in concert with Philippine President Manuel Roxas.

As it were, Russell Volckmann and Manuel Roxas had forged a close friendship during the darkest days of the guerrilla campaign in North Luzon. Now that Roxas had been elected President of the Philippines, he and Volckmann produced an amnesty proclamation that read, "Any act performed in furtherance of the resistance movement should be exonerated." While the amnesty act proved beneficial to the Americans (indeed, no American ever came to trial), it had mixed results for the Filipinos. Several Filipinos were being pulled into the court system, which cost the Philippine government more time and money than it could feasibly devote to the project. Subsequently, President Roxas created "amnesty boards," that travelled around the country to hear the charges levied against Filipino men and officers. Amnesty boards were unique because they did not require a lawyer and, initially, fell beyond the country's jurisprudence. The accused would go before the board, plead their case, and "if it looked as though their actions were in furtherance of the resistance movement, amnesty was granted."

But the amnesty system was flawed and rather ambiguous. For example, if a Filipino were charged with executing a certain collaborator and replied "Yes, I did it because he was an informer," then that was enough to exonerate him. If, however, he said "I was directed to execute him by Captain John Smith [hypothetical name]. I was carrying out his orders," or some other phraseology, the case would be thrown to the Philippine courts. Under that system, many former Philippine guerrillas ended up in prison, although some were never convicted legally.

Nearly a decade later, however, the matter came to the attention of the new Philippine President, Ramon Magsaysay. Magsaysay himself had been a guerrilla in Western Luzon and, upon hearing of the legal plights of his comrades, he immediately sprang into action. All cases were reopened and accompanied by fact-finding missions to determine whether the incarcerated guerrillas had acted on the orders of an American officer. Magsaysay, however, was not oblivious to the darker side of human nature. He conceded that some of the Philippine guerrillas had used the war as an opportunity to eliminate their personal enemies. Thus, Magsaysay's task was to separate fact from fiction, separating the murderers from those who had killed in the line of duty. Under the Magsaysay project, some latter-day guerrillas eventually regained their freedom.

With his new bride, Jay Vanderpool returned to the US in February 1947. In light of his experience as an Allied guerrilla liaison and Division G-2, Vanderpool was assigned to the newly-created Central Intelligence Group (CIG), the forerunner to the modern-day CIA.

The CIG had grown out of the former Office of Strategic Services (OSS). During World War II, the OSS had been America's premier intelligence agency. Headed by Major General William "Wild Bill" Donovan, the OSS coordinated all levels of espionage behind enemy lines for every branch of the US Military—including propaganda and subversion. Prior to formation of the OSS, the FBI and each branch of the military had its own intelligence apparatus—and they rarely spoke to one another. Donovan recognized, however, that the perennial stove-piping of intelligence was inefficient and counter-productive. In November 1944, he penned a letter to President Roosevelt, outlining the need for a peacetime "Central Intelligence Service" that could "procure intelligence both by overt and covert methods and will at the same time provide intelligence guidance, determine national intelligence objectives, and correlate the intelligence material collected by all government agencies."

Following FDR's death, however, President Truman dismantled the OSS, and the FBI began to position itself as America's next foreign intelligence service. In place of the OSS, however, Truman created the National Intelligence Authority (NIA), whose operational arm was the CIG. And when Truman signed the National Security Act in September 1947, the CIG and NIA were rolled into the newly-dubbed "Central Intelligence Agency."

When Vanderpool arrived at CIG Headquarters, he remembered it being a time of flux for the US military. "I was working then as the CIG Army liaison—more of a messenger, I think, than anything else—on the reorganization of national defense in 1947." The War Department had now morphed into the "Department of

Defense;" the latter-day Army Air Forces had become their own separate branch of the service; and the racial desegregation of America's military was close at hand.

Moreover, these were the inaugural years of the burgeoning "Cold War." It was to be fought not necessarily with bombs and bullets, but with words and ideas. The "hot" battles would be fought largely by proxy at the farthest corners of the earth. Words like "Mutual Assured Destruction;" "Nuclear Holocaust;" and "Balance of Power" would steer the course of American foreign policy for the next forty-five years.

As it turned out, Vanderpool's assignment to the CIA would revolve around the first "hotspot" of the Cold War: the Korean Peninsula. "The CIA needed someone to go out to Korea who knew a little about Asia," Jay recalled. Having spent his formative years in the Army fighting the Japanese, and then navigating the gunpoint diplomacy of occupation duty, the CIA selected Jay Vanderpool to represent them in Korea.

Korea had been a Japanese colony from its annexation in 1910 until the end of World War II. Following the Allied victory, the United States and the Soviet Union divided the peninsula into two political zones along the 38th Parallel. Subsequently, the north became a Communist state while the south remained capitalist. The Soviets and Americans withdrew from their sectors in 1948 and 1949, respectively. But both superpowers continued to support their client states on either side of the 38th Parallel.

Meanwhile, Kim Il-sung, the inaugural dictator of North Korea, founded the Korean People's Army (KPA). Encompassing all branches of the military (including ground, naval, and air forces), the KPA drew its ranks from a cadre of guerrillas and former soldiers who had fought against the Japanese and Nationalist Chinese forces. As such, the first iteration of KPA ground forces were highly skilled in infiltration tactics and guerrilla warfare. Along with a steady stream of Soviet advisors, Joseph Stalin equipped Kim's forces with a generous arsenal of Soviet equipment. And Kim Il-sung was determined to reunify the Korean Peninsula by force if necessary.

The seemingly-unchecked growth in North Korea's military capabilities, however, had gotten the attention of nearly everyone in the Pentagon. "The problem," said Jay, "was that President Truman was not satisfied with the current estimate of the North Korean military forces." Indeed, no one in the Allied intelligence community could agree on just how big the KPA had become. "The British and Chinese were pretty well-agreed that there were about 35,000 or 36,000 trained troops in North Korea," he continued. General MacArthur's G-2, however, estimated the KPA strength to be about 136,000. Irritated by the conflicting reports, President Truman turned to the CIA and said: "What is the damn story?! Send someone over there to find out and let me know the facts!"

Jay Vanderpool was the chosen one.

It remains unclear, however, why the CIA tapped Vanderpool for the mission. The Agency already had a sizeable field operation in Japan and South Korea. Perhaps Truman and the CIA's top brass saw Vanderpool as an independent auditor who could give expert reconnaissance, and provide an unbiased assessment free from the CIA's intra-agency politics. Jay was, after all, *detailed* to the CIA as a military attaché. He did not technically belong to the Agency.

Within days, he had arrived in Japan for his mission brief, presumably speaking with MacArthur's G-2, before landing in South Korea en route to the borderlands of the 38th Parallel. "I was out there about two months," he said, before he could determine the size and disposition of the KPA. He never gave the details of *how* he gathered his intelligence data, but sufficed to say he spent considerable time sneaking around the Korean countryside, observing various posts and speaking with verified human "sources" within the CIA's network of friendly spooks.

From his own data, Vanderpool estimated the KPA strength at only 36,000.

"MacArthur's staff estimate was in error," said Jay.

Indeed, Vanderpool's numbers were more than 100,000 below the end-strengths projected by MacArthur's General Staff. Once Jay was certain that his numbers were correct, he recorded the data onto his Top Secret One-Time Pad—an encryption tool wherein plaintext was paired to a pre-shared cryptological key, and "of which there were only three copies in the world: the President had one, CIA had one, and I had one." Jay's estimates were confirmed by the US 14th Corps' G-2 (North Korean Intelligence Section).

Jay prepared his report and presented it to the 14th Corps commander, Lieutenant General John Hodges. "Sir, I can't give this to anyone except you," said Jay, "but I want you to see that I'm not going to say anything without your knowledge." Hodges thanked him for the report and filed it accordingly.

"From then on," he continued, "I did routine spy-chasing work around there like most of the hoods do." By the time Vanderpool had arrived in Korea, however, the CIA was battling its own spotty track record. The fall of Czechoslovakia and Romania to the Soviets; the Berlin Blockade; and the treachery of double agent Kim Philby were all (unfairly or not), charged as failures of the CIA.

Moreover, South Korea was teeming with Communist spies. Vanderpool himself gained a more intimate knowledge of the Korean terrain "from travelling around, chasing agents in and out," intercepting Soviet, Red Chinese, and North Korean agents on a regular basis.

In the spring of 1950, his tour with the CIA came to an end. "I was on my way home to go to school at Fort Sill, Oklahoma." In a peculiar turn of events, Vanderpool was ordered to attend the Field Artillery Officer Advanced Course (FAOAC). Fort Sill had long been home to the Field Artillery School—the point of entry for most of the US Army's artillery soldiers and officers. During the prewar years, some artillerymen like Vanderpool had evaded the schoolhouse at Fort Sill by taking their recruit training at in-house facilities at places like Schofield Barracks. But now as an officer in the postwar Army, he was expected to take his formal Continuing Ed courses at Fort Sill.

Although the course was designed to prepare junior captains for battery command, Vanderpool knew he would benefit from attending. Like many World War II veterans, he had the option of using his combat experience as "constructive credit" for the Army Service Schools. After all, his wartime on-the-job training in combat had given him more experience than most officers would see in twenty years of peacetime service.

But, as a Lieutenant Colonel, Jay Vanderpool enrolled in a class filled with young captains.

It was an eight-month course of study, and a worthwhile opportunity to learn the "nitty-gritty" of battery-level tactics and manipulating artillery fires directly from the gunline.

But as Jay Vanderpool departed Korea for the wind-swept plains of his native Oklahoma, Kim Il-sung was making his final preparations for war. With the goal of reuniting the Korean Peninsula under Communist rule, the KPA stormed across the 38th Parallel on June 25, 1950.

6

This Kind of War

The conflict was unique for the US military because it wasn't a "war" in the traditional sense—there had been no formal declaration of hostilities; and it was the first conflict carried out under the banner of the United Nations (UN). President Harry Truman therefore dubbed it a "police action." At first glance, however, it appeared that the conflict was a minor adjunct of World War II. The military used much of the same weaponry and tactics as it had during the previous war. At the higher echelons, Korea featured much of the same cast from World War II. General Douglas MacArthur, former commander of the Southwest Pacific Area, returned as commander-in-chief of UN forces in Korea. General Omar Bradley was now Chairman of the Joint Chiefs; and General J. Lawton Collins, who had commanded the 25th Infantry Division in the Pacific (and later, the VII Corps in Europe), was now the Army Chief of Staff. Lieutenant General Matthew Ridgway, an airborne pioneer and former commander of the 82nd Airborne Division, returned as commander of the US Eighth Army.

Although the invasion took the US by surprise, many predicted that Korea would be an easy victory. MacArthur cheerfully surmised that his troops would be home by Christmas 1950. Others thought that the North Koreans would simply quit the field as soon as they realized they were fighting Americans. After all, the US had just defeated Germany and Japan—who were the North Koreans to tussle with America's war machine?

However, the Army of 1950 was a far cry from the eight-million-man force that had defeated the Nazis five years earlier. Training and readiness sank to an all-time low as the US demobilized its army and discharged their wartime conscripts. By 1949, a soldier's typical day consisted of little more than constabulary duty, organized athletics, and USO dances. Thus, in the opening stages of the war, the US paid a terrible price for its unpreparedness.

After a disastrous encounter at the Battle of Osan, the atrophied American forces retreated south to the port of Pusan, where they rallied to make their final stand against the KPA. For six weeks spanning August-September 1950, the UN troops (consisting mostly of American, British, and South Korean forces) beat back the North Korean assault in what became known as the "Pusan Perimeter"—a 140-mile defensive line around the city. After a miraculous break-out from Pusan, and the simultaneous Allied landing at Inchon, the Americans rallied a counteroffensive which pushed the North Koreans back across the 38th Parallel and as far north as the Yalu River.

"I was in Hong Kong when the war broke out," said Jay, enjoying an exotic layover ahead of his reporting date to Fort Sill. Since General Collins, his former division commander, was now the Chief of Staff, Jay was certain that he'd let him go back to Korea.

"So, I sent him a message."

After all, Collins had first-hand knowledge of Vanderpool's exploits throughout the Pacific. And Jay was quick to point out his more recent experience alongside the CIA, drawing useful information about the enemy spy networks along the Korean Peninsula. Surely, Collins would agree that Jay was of better use to the Army on the frontlines in Korea than within the sterile confines of the schoolhouse.

Sadly, it was not to be.

"He declined and told me to go to school," said Jay, that there was nothing I could do there that MacArthur couldn't do better."

Thus, Jay reported to Fort Sill for his eight-month enrollment at FAOAC. However, it wouldn't be long before he found himself back in action. Upon graduating from the Advanced Course, Jay was re-assigned to the Far East Command as the Chief of Intelligence for the General Headquarters. These G-2 assignments, however, had become a recurring theme in his career. Although the G-2 staff provided actionable intelligence, their daily duties revolved around a tedious schedule of paperwork and clerical tasks. All told, Jay felt he could serve the Army better if he were closer to the front lines.

Meanwhile, following the breakout from the Pusan Perimeter, UN forces had the North Koreans on their heels and, for a while, it appeared that the war was in its last throes—until the Communist Chinese entered the fight. Beginning in the fall of 1950, the Chinese counteroffensive regained much of the land that had been lost to UN forces following the Inchon landings. Indeed, by January 1951, the Communists had re-occupied Seoul and pushed the UN as far south as Wongju, where the frontlines had stabilized. However, during their blitzkrieg to Seoul, the Chinese had outrun their supply lines, allowing the UN to regain the initiative and rollback the Communist tide through a series of counterattacks including Operation Roundup, Operation Killer, and Operation Ripper—the latter of which expelled the Communists from Seoul.

That spring, the Chinese attempted one more counteroffensive before being halted by the US X Corps in May 1951. By month's end, the Eighth US Army counterattacked and re-established the frontlines just north of the 38th Parallel. For the remaining two years of the war, the UN Command and the Red Chinese continued fighting, but exchanged little ground.

For Jay Vanderpool, however, Korea gave him the opportunity to participate in the burgeoning field of "special forces operations." Throughout the conflict, Allied unconventional warfare occurred in two overlapping phases. During the first phase (spanning from June 1950 until the fall of 1951), US conventional forces conducted counter-guerrilla operations against the KPA irregulars. The second phase of unconventional warfare (from January 1951 until the cease-fire in 1953) saw the US Eighth Army develop its own "special operations command" to conduct guerrilla warfare behind enemy lines. The North Koreans, given their recent experience fighting the Japanese and Nationalist Chinese, made extensive use of guerrilla warfare during the inaugural years of the Korean Conflict. From a military standpoint, Communist guerillas served two functions: first, their tactics could offset the superiority of American maneuver forces; and second, while camouflaging themselves within the local population, Communist partisans could work to undermine American ideologies.

The geopolitical irony of the situation was not lost on men like Jay Vanderpool. Indeed, the KPA strategies were nearly identical to those used by the latter-day Allied guerrillas in the Philippines. As North Korean partisans continued wreaking havoc on the UN's rear echelons, Army Chief of Staff General Collins, scrambled for a plan to neutralize the enemy guerrillas. His hastily-devised solution, however, included a directive to all in-theater units (as well as those tapped for deployment) to receive instruction on counter-guerrilla techniques. General MacArthur, meanwhile, from his perch as the UN commander, authorized the creation of special anti-guerrilla units.

As it turned out, the US Army had no regular command structure for special operations. In fact, the term "special operations" had yet to gain widespread acceptance throughout the military. In response to North Korean partisans, the Army simply created a series of *ad hoc* units geared for counter-guerrilla or "behind-the-lines" activities. Most of these units fell under jurisdiction of the Eighth Army's G-3 Miscellaneous Group.[11]

Colonel John H. McGee, another veteran of the Philippine Campaign, became the inaugural Director of Special Operations for the Eighth Army. Under McGee's leadership, the Eighth Army organized and led numerous teams of South Korean (and disaffected North Korean) partisans behind enemy lines. Throughout its existence, this "guerrilla command" went by several names—including: the Attrition Section; the 8086th Army Unit; the 8240th Army Unit; and the United Nations Partisan Forces Korea (UNPFK). By the summer of 1951, McGee had established two permanent guerrilla bases, several mobile bases, and a cadre for training Korean agents for covert missions. McGee then passed his command of the Eighth Army guerrillas to Lieutenant Colonel Samuel W. Koster.[12]

According to Vanderpool, however, Sam Koster had gradually soured on the partisan duty, and preferred a General Headquarters assignment. "I negotiated a deal with [Koster] who had the partisan job, who didn't like it, and I had the G-2 job I didn't like, so arrangements were made for us to swap places. That's how I got to Korea again."

When Vanderpool arrived to take command of the partisan operations in December 1951, the unit was being redesignated as the

8240th Army Unit (AU). "They called them *partisans*," he noted, "not guerrillas." Moreover, the top brass insisted that all "partisans" be referred to as "UN" assets. But whatever their designation, Vanderpool noted that the 8240th personnel were tough, capable, and fiercely anti-Communist. "The partisans were made up primarily of people with military training in the Japanese Army, the Korean Army, the Chinese Army, or some other army. At the battalion level, there were political leaders . . . mayors of cities, superintendents of schools, the intellectual leaders of their communities," said Vanderpool. He noticed that many of these partisan battalions were akin to the Army National Guard units he had seen throughout World War II. The Korean partisans within a certain battalion often came from the same town. Their battalion leadership consisted of the same community leaders they had known for most of their lives—"the mayor, the police chief . . . or someone like that." As Jay recalled, this gave them a good sense of kinship and a motivation to perform well. Since many of them had undergone basic military training in one army or another, they all had solid foundations upon which to carry out their duties. And since many of them had been Chinese and North Korean defectors, they could offer valuable insights into the enemy's culture and tactics.

"What they lacked," said Jay, "was equipment, communication, and organization." Despite John McGee's initial progress in organizing these UN partisan forces, there was much work to be done. For instance, when Vanderpool arrived at the 8240th, he noticed that the partisans were carrying Soviet-made rifles and machine guns. "This is fine when you are on the offensive and you are capturing materiel," he said, "but when your lines go static, you're no longer capturing equipment. The ammunition was being used up, the rifles worn out, and no replacements."

Thus, Jay Vanderpool brokered a deal with the CIA.

At the time, whenever a replacement soldier arrived in Korea, he was issued a rifle in-theater. When the soldier redeployed, however, he would have to surrender his rifle to the armory. "By normal replacement, we had tens of thousands of rifles, stacked up in protective grease somewhere." Meanwhile, the CIA desperately wanted to issue Soviet-built rifles to their field agents. "They wanted the Russian weapons [in their field offices] in other parts of the world," he said. "I made a deal that we'd give the partisans the American rifles and machine guns and we would turn in all of our captured Russian and Chinese equipment. With that, we started building a combat force—we had a really good company-level, battalion-level training program. I started off with around five or six thousand partisans, and slowly built them up to about 21,000."

Initially, the 8240th AU's sector comprised the western coast of the peninsula, starting from Inchon in the south, to as far northward as they were brave enough to go.[13] "At that time, the CIA was controlling the partisans in northeast Korea, in the mountains, up near Russia. The X Corps was running some operations on the east coast without much coordination really." Although UN partisan forces were internally re-structured at various times throughout the war, they generally took the shape of a regimental or brigade-sized task force.

"The biggest unit we had," said Jay, "was a rifle battalion . . . it was very similar to the Philippines where we had worked with a vast number of individual leaders. The system we set up was this: At the regimental level we installed American officers. We gave them a staff that was American heavy, with Korean assistants. At the battalion level . . . commanders were Korean, with American advisors. Companies had Korean commanders with a few American advisors. Then, as a matter of course, these people had very tight territorial interests near their homes, so you could not move them too far from their hometowns. This of course was because they had to feed their families and they didn't receive any pay. The partisans didn't draw any salary, and that was not always considered by higher headquarters. They had to have some way they could get to their families to feed them."

Apart from their coastal areas, the UN partisans occupied a number of offshore islands near the 38th Parallel (and along the western edges of North Korea's territorial waters). The KPA in turn spent much of the war trying to drive the guerrillas from the occupied islands. But Vanderpool's guerrillas and their American advisors were never alone on these islands. At any one time, each of the island citadels were supported by CIA personnel; Allied radar detachments; US Air Force Search & Rescue Teams; Allied helicopter rescue detachments; counterintelligence teams; ROK Marines and naval personnel; air defense batteries; and US naval gunfire liaisons.

And it was from these island bases that Vanderpool's guerrillas launched many of their most successful operations. "We didn't have any landing boats," he said, "so we got a whole bunch of Korean fishing boats, Chinese Junks, etc." Each boat was modified with its own American engine. "First, we installed the Grey 225 marine engine," Jay recalled. When the guerrillas had no more Grey engines to spare, "we started putting in General Motors truck engines. We had to cast our own screws and make our own shafts. We converted most of the boats into powered boats."

For the next sixteen months, Jay Vanderpool commanded the partisans' daily activities "and was directly responsible for all guerrilla operations, training, and administration." His presence gave the guerrillas (and their advisors) the stability and leadership they needed. Moreover, Jay insulated his partisans from the perennial indecision and lack of direction from the higher echelons. In the absence of formal guidance from higher headquarters, Jay Vanderpool took the initiative and made decisions without looking back. In fact, Major Richard Ripley, one of Jay's subordinates in the 8240th, clearly recalled that "the only operational guidance I received came from Vanderpool."

In fact, Jay Vanderpool proved himself to be the right man for the job. Like John McGee before him, Vanderpool gave "clear guidance and direction that shaped how the guerrillas trained, planned, and conducted their operations." To that end, he developed two critical planning documents.

The first document, issued in April 1952, was known simply as: *Guerrilla Operations Outline 1952*. As a directive to his subordinate task force commanders, the *Guerrilla Operations Outline* provided a "broad guidance on tactics, operations, air and naval support, prioritization of targets, and other pertinent issues" upon which the partisans would synchronize and standardize their efforts. But, as Vanderpool recalled, his directive was intended for use "as a guide, rather than a restriction" on how the 8240th conducted its operations. Thus, it showed that Jay trusted the tactical decision-making of his subordinates, and encouraged them to take initiative within the bounds of generally-defined guidelines.

And, just as he had done with his Filipino guerrillas, he advised the Korean partisans to "avoid trying to win the war by yourself." He likewise cautioned that, if the enemy were to gain an advantage during a firefight, the partisans were expected to "get away to fight another day." Standing toe-to-toe against the Red Chinese or KPA would not end well for the UN guerrillas. "Hit and run," he said, "those are guerrilla tactics," and "Substitute speed and surprise for mass."

The second document was addendum and revision to the Far East Command's Operations Plan (OPLAN) for Guerrilla Warfare. Within his revisions to the existing OPLAN, Vanderpool specified the "missions, tasks, and special planning considerations" for each of the partisan elements under his command. Subsequently, their mission sets would revolve around two kinds of tactical operations: *raids* and *mobile defenses*.

"I liked the raids," said Vanderpool, "because we could really hurt the enemy by going after radar and radio stations." But what his men enjoyed most about these raids was the gastronomic windfall they would often find—including stockpiles of North Korean rice, salt, and oxen. Under the Rules of Engagement, UN troops could keep any foodstuffs or livestock seized during a raid. "They could either eat or sell them, whatever they wanted to do." In a practical way, this alleviated much of the post-WWII hunger problems that had plagued rural South Koreans since 1945. The partisans, after collecting their newfound pantry items, often sold the salt to buy fish and vegetables for their families.

Naturally, "it was a very popular operation," Jay recalled.

Livestock was another priority target during these raids. "You could tie a rope around the cow's horns," he said, "and tie them to the gunwale of your boat to keep their noses above the water." Surprisingly, the local bovines could survive in the water for nearly 30 to 40 miles offshore without drowning—"but in very cold weather they suffered."

Still, commandeering cattle was no easy feat. Thus, according to Vanderpool: "We'd wait until harvest was just under way, or everyone was out plowing." Thus, a raiding party of guerrillas would come ashore with two or three thousand men, "round up all the oxen and take them out of the fields." As Vanderpool noted: "That stopped the rice planting." With their draft animals gone, the enemy farms began to suffer, and so too did the enemy's food network.

The UN partisans, meanwhile, were delighted that they could feed their families—"which they couldn't do before." As the partisans began raiding more farms and food depots, the Far East Command G-4 granted Jay permission to feed his men two *Go* of rice per day. A *Go* was an Asian unit of volume equivalent to 100 milliliters or 2/5 of a metric cup. Each partisan was given two *Go* of rice daily. "Why two *Go*? Because they could use one *Go* to eat, and one *Go* to swap for vegetables and fish, meat, things like that. So, at times they were pretty well-fed. The families were better off than they would have been without it."

Gastronomic rewards notwithstanding, Jay recalled that: "Our raids were well-supported. We had a couple of British Navy cruisers and several destroyers that supported us with gunfire. We normally had at least one US aircraft carrier to give us backup aircraft support. We could hit the beach and make a raid, covered by fire, and get out with negligible casualties." Although he found his guerrillas to be excellent at defensive operations, the raids allowed them to flex their short-range offensive skills. "For limited offensives up to a few thousand meters," Jay recalled, "they were very good . . . because they knew how to use the bayonet, rifle and hand grenade; therefore, we were able to carry out some pretty credible military operations." Indeed, the 8240th AU could put a raiding party of 2,000–3,000 men ashore within half an hour. "We kept this fleet up until the end of the war, or until the time I left [in the spring of 1953], when things were slowing down. We would actually lift about four or five thousand men, simultaneously, in small craft carrying up to platoon-size forces."

On other occasions, these raids came to resemble "search-and-destroy" missions. Citing one such example, Jay recalled that: "On the Yalu River, there was a big radar net along the [mountainous] ridgeline on the east bank of the river." These interconnected radar stations had been causing trouble for the Far East Command because they could track UN flights from Seoul all the way to Gimpo Air Base along the 38th Parallel. "The Air Force wanted to know if we could knock those radars out. I was given the task to see what I might do about it."

As such, Jay rounded up three airborne guerrilla companies who had just finished their basic parachute training. "I think they had three jumps each," he said. "They were already infantry trained," and Jay started preparing them for company-and-platoon-sized raiding operations.

However, Jay decided to add his own touch of psychological warfare.

While down in Pusan, he came across an interesting discovery at the UN refugee center—"somebody had brought in a whole bunch of Nazi paratrooper uniforms from World War II: caps, beautiful boots, peg trousers. They were stacked all over the place."

But seeing the finely-pressed Nazi regalia gave him an idea.

"I had girls in the sewing loft who could make all of our own copied uniforms for any army in the world. If we had a sample, we could copy it."[14] Thus, Jay Vanderpool dressed his parachute commandos in a slew of meticulously-reconstructed Nazi uniforms. And he marveled at the thought of how frightened (and confused) the enemy radar operators would be upon seeing a team of Nazi paratroopers descending onto their stations.

Two companies ultimately made the jump onto the enemy ridgeline. "They hit those radar stations in the middle of the night," he said. Meanwhile, Vanderpool's liaisons in the Army Security Agency (the organization responsible for intercepting and monitoring enemy signals traffic), deciphered the Chinese mayday calls from the radar stations during the attack. True to Vanderpool's instincts, the Chinese radar technicians were in full panic, thinking they were truly under attack from Nazi stormtroopers. "It was three or four days before they got over the shock," he said.

More importantly, however, Vanderpool's men knocked out every radar atop that ridge. Looking back on that raid, however, Jay realized he had given his commandos too much extraneous equipment. In most military circles, the attitude towards mission equipment was: "It's better to have it and not need it, than need it and not have it." But for this nighttime raid, "the partisans had a lot of explosives they had not used," Jay remembered. "Many of them got hurt by staying too long, having fun cutting railroad tracks, blowing up bridges. It doesn't do much good cutting tracks, which somebody will repair in 12 hours." The partisans also used their bazookas to target enemy locomotives, of which they killed several. But, as Jay admitted, the guerrillas often got so caught up in the thrill of their killing spree, that they "wouldn't come out on time." Indeed, whenever the guerrillas remained on a target area for too long, they gave the enemy more time to regain the initiative and launch counterattacks. "When they stayed too long," he said, "they usually got hurt." Still, neither the Communists nor UN forces could deny the effectiveness of the partisan troops. The guerrillas were, as Vanderpool described them, "extending the left flank of the Eighth Army around the coastlines."

Jay was equally impressed by their ability to conduct defensive operations. "An example of our defensive missions," he said, "is illustrated by the night battle at Sunwi-do. Our control of offshore islands was a considerable annoyance to the Communist forces. Sunwi-do was a very small island, some 4,000–5,000 meters offshore, northwest of Seoul. We kept a reinforced partisan battalion there and ran raids over to the mainland to annoy the enemy." The KPA, meanwhile, had built up a task force of more than 3,000 troops to crush the guerrillas on Sunwi-do. Like the Americans, the North Koreans calculated their amphibious operations by the rise and fall of the tides.

And along the western coast of Korea, the tides could be viciously strong.

In fact, Vanderpool recalled that 25-foot tide surges were not uncommon.

"One night when low tide would be about midnight," said Jay, "the North Koreans started a force of 3,000-plus men to attack across the mud flats and take Sunwi-do." The guerrillas, however, detected the incoming attack and opened fire at long range with mortars and machine guns. "We had deployed a line of 55-gallon drums filled with napalm to be ignited by wires from the island." As the enemy began to buckle under the machine gun fire, the sudden burst of napalm sent them into a scattered frenzy. "A small force actually came ashore," he admitted, "but was driven back."

By 10:00 PM, American fighter-bombers had descended onto Sunwi-do, ready to strafe the fledgling enemy troops along the surf. The guerrillas were holding the beach brilliantly against the KPA when the Air Force dropped its first round of parachute flares and began their strafing runs. "The North Koreans decided just before midnight to pull back," said Jay, "but were still illuminated by the flares and pinned down by aircraft."

The KPA's timing, however, was their last fatal mistake.

"They were caught by the incoming tide shortly after midnight," he said. And the raging tide took many of the North Korean raiders to their deaths. "It was cold that night—below zero," Jay continued. "The water was full of chunks of flow ice. Most of the North Koreans were caught by the 20-plus feet of ice water." The fighter-bombers withdrew once they no longer detected any movement along the mud flats. "A series of aerial photographs were taken by parachute flare light. The Air Force photo interpreters said later they had counted about 3,000 enemy soldiers on the mud flats or in the ice water. The next morning at daylight, and on a high tide, the British Navy sent combat vessels through the channel looking for survivors. None were found. Neither the North Koreans nor the Chinese ever tried that maneuver again."

While most of these iconic missions occurred along the west coast of Korea, the 8240th AU likewise established a partisan presence along the eastern coast. But, as Vanderpool conceded, they never mustered as many guerrillas to the eastern shores as they did to the west. "We could only get up to three or four battalions operating over there," he said. "The war was slowing down; also, we didn't have the offshore bases on the east coast we could hold for sustained operations."

Still, Jay Vanderpool was immensely pleased by how well the guerrilla campaign had played out. Their greatest accomplishment, he said, was "keeping the enemy off balance." The hit-and-run, harassment techniques kept the North Koreans and Red Chinese well-distracted and tactically hamstrung along the UN front. "The partisans couldn't whip the Chinese," he conceded, "who were better equipped, but they could whip the North Koreans. The partisans just didn't have the fire power or organization to fight the Chinese the way the Americans could; but it kept them [the Chinese] off balance. It denied them local food for their troops and for their people."[15]

That said, however, the UN guerrilla operations did not always go smoothly. In fact, the manner by which the Army had approached unconventional warfare was largely *ad hoc*—they had thrown together a "special operations command" for the occasion. Some observers noted that the Army needed a permanent command structure for unconventional warfare. This was one of the intellectual seeds that gave rise to the modern-day Special Forces.

And although the UN partisans achieved numerous tactical victories, some critics noted that the guerrillas' operational focus (and their skill sets) were too narrow. Statistically speaking, the UN guerrillas had amassed an impressive record: By the end of 1951, they had killed more than 9,000 enemy troops; captured nearly 400 enemy prisoners; destroyed and/or impounded more than 800 pieces of enemy equipment, and claimed the destruction of 49 bridges and 22 railroads. But more than half of their engagements had been in open combat against enemy forces. Conversely, only *eleven percent* of their activity had been dedicated to sabotage. As Colonel Rod Paschall poignantly remarked, "the partisans had devoted most of their energy and efforts into killing the troops of an enemy that had an almost inexhaustible supply of manpower." Meanwhile, the task of cultivating civilian support was left to conventional assets and third-party civil agencies (e.g. UN Civil Assistance Command).

Also, guerrilla operations depended heavily on naval support and seaborne delivery into their areas of operation. These conditions effectively put the guerrillas on a "coastal tether," and potentially put their operations at the mercy of competing naval requirements.

Reflecting on his personal experiences, however, Vanderpool was grateful to have forged close partnerships (and later, close friendships) with a number of South Korean military giants. Prior to the war, when Vanderpool had been detailed to the CIA, he established a cross-cultural rapport with General Chae Byung Duk, the ROK Army Chief of Staff. The general referred to himself as "Fat Chae" because, as Jay noted, "he was quite chubby." Despite Chae's girth, however, Jay acknowledged that he was a tremendously talented officer. Chae's only professional handicap was that he couldn't speak English. Naturally, the language barrier and perennial need for an interpreter hamstrung his interactions with other Allied leaders.

Vanderpool also forged a close relationship with Chae's G-2, Paik Sun Yup. Paik later became the ROK Army Chief of Staff after General Chae was killed during an assault. Chae prided himself on being a "fighting general," and insisted that he share the burdens of combat with his men. Vanderpool, recalling Chae's demise, said: "It was an assault going up a hill and he got carried away. He took his pistol and rifle . . . went up with the troops and got killed." Paik and Vanderpool had worked together during the latter's tour in the CIA; and Paik became the Chief of Staff just in time to receive Vanderpool as the incoming commander of UN partisan forces. Thus, when Vanderpool returned to Korea for the shooting war, "I had a ready-made entree to the Korean people through the military, through General Paik, who had worked with me when I was there before." This partnership was critical to the guerrilla's success, said Vanderpool, as they provided expert trainers and advisors to the 8240th AU. "For example, if I needed a good specialist in training, they could get me one out of the [ROK] army, and loan him to me for a month or two," to render any variety of training expertise to the UN partisans—be it demolitions, indirect fires, or night fighting techniques.

By April 1953, when Jay Vanderpool relinquished his command of the UN partisans, the Korean Conflict was slowly grinding to a halt. Less than three weeks following the Battle of Pork Chop Hill, the negotiating parties at Panmunjom finally reached an accord. The resulting armistice—signed on July 27, 1953—restored the international boundary at the 38th Parallel, reverted both countries to the *status quo antebellum*, and established the Korean Demilitarized Zone (DMZ). After the demarcation agreement, the US kept a permanent military presence along the DMZ to deter any further aggression.

Vanderpool and many of his comrades, however, felt that the US had sabotaged its own success. Although the US had declared victory, they had essentially fought the Communists to a draw. The enemy had dictated the tempo for most of the war and the Army's rules of engagement tended to discourage initiative rather than promote it. Among the conventional frontline forces, a company commander's actions frequently had to get approval from as high as division-level. To the rank-and-file soldiers, the war's objectives were unclear and seemingly changed from day to day. There seemed to be no reason why the UN forces would suddenly seize a hill, boast about "pushing back" the Red Chinese, and then suddenly abandon the hill with virtually no explanation. Furthermore, it seemed that the political and higher-echelon leadership didn't have the same desire for "absolute victory" that they had had in World War II. On the conventional front, and in the realm of special operations, men like Jay Vanderpool felt that the Korean War might have taken a better trajectory had it not been for the Pentagon's heavy-handed interference. Yet Vanderpool remained optimistic that America's next conflict—wherever it may be—would be fought on better terms.

7

Winged Sabers

When Jay Vanderpool returned from Korea, he was looking forward to a stateside assignment and, hopefully, a longer stretch of peacetime. By the summer of 1953, he and Lynn had been married for six years. Yet because of Jay's deployment tempo, the young couple had spent only about half of those six years together. Now, they were eagerly looking forward to spending more time together as a couple.

"When I finished up in Korea," he said, "I was ordered to Camp Polk, Louisiana, to assume command of one or more artillery battalions." Camp Polk, however, was among the least desirable of the Army's stateside posts. Even after the Army declared Camp Polk to be a "permanent installation," thus elevating it to the status of "Fort Polk," it did nothing to improve the post's overall reputation. Nestled among the swamps of Louisiana, and far from any major metro areas, it seemed that a soldiers' only reliable companions at Fort Polk would be the alligators and mosquitos. In the coming decades, soldiers would often refer to Polk as the "armpit of the Army;" and some would spend their entire careers trying to avoid an assignment there.

Still, his assignment to the Bayou State gave him a chance to return to his core competencies as an artilleryman. He was about to take command of *three* different artillery battalions. They were short of lieutenant colonels and majors to command," he recalled, "so one had to command three or four [battalions] individually, with separate staffs." In practice, commanding three simultaneous battalions essentially made Vanderpool a brigade commander.

It was another opportunity to punch above his weight class.

It was, however, an Army returning to the lighter, leaner days of the post-World War II era. Granted, the Army's overall readiness was comparatively better than it had been in 1949, but the mid-1950s were marked by an emphasis on strategic retaliation and nuclear deterrence. The reliance on long-range and tactical nuclear forces, however, had drawn funding away from conventional ground forces. And, like every unit in the Army (in war and peacetime) Vanderpool's unit had its mix of "good men and some not so very good." To round out the metaphysical mix of personnel, Vanderpool recalled: "We consolidated the [high-performing] people into one really good battalion at the cost of trying to run three or four separate half-strength battalions." Then, the under-performing battalions could be augmented by competent replacements. "In so doing," Jay continued, "I developed a pretty good cadre."

His lateral command of multiple battalions was also a crash course in racial integration. President Truman had integrated the US Armed Forces six years earlier; now black soldiers and white soldiers were serving alongside each other. To Jay Vanderpool, however, integration was nothing new. He had served alongside Filipinos and Koreans under the worst of wartime conditions. Taking command of an officially de-segregated unit, however, provided the basis for a great sociological experiment. At first, nearly all of his soldiers were black. When the first wave of replacements came in, most of the incoming soldiers were white or Hispanic. Vanderpool couldn't help but notice the disparity in their comparative education levels. The current cadre of enlisted men had about six to eight years of formal education. Nearly all the incoming soldiers (including many peacetime draftees), however, had high school diplomas and one year of college. "So, this gives a very interesting sociological experiment of integration in reverse, shall we say."

As such, Vanderpool and his officers hoarded the battalions into the base theater. "We discussed integration at great length," he said, "because it was to the advantage of these black sergeants to make this thing work as well for them as for me as a commander."

And it worked.

"We never had one racial incident for the next several years," he beamed.

In a similar vein, Jay remarked that his African-American soldiers were among the best he had ever commanded. "I picked the wisest and best one . . . to be sergeant major of the battalion. He said he didn't want the job; I told him I didn't want mine either, but we both had them. Sergeant Lee and his wife Audrey had a fine family. This all worked to make this thing succeed and we had one of the best relationships of any outfit I've ever been in."

For the next several months, Vanderpool trained his battalions and was able to validate their collective proficiency up through the battery level. "We had not started battalion-level [training] when I got orders to march the battalion to Fort Campbell, Kentucky . . . to be attached to the 11th Airborne Division. We marched up to Kentucky, where we spent the next several months going through advanced battery and battalion training, battalion tests, etc."

Around this time, Vanderpool began to take note of the happenings in Indochina. The entire region had been a French colony from 1887 until the rise of the Viet Minh Independence Movement led by Ho

Chi Minh in the 1940s. During World War II, Ho Chi Minh had rescued several downed American pilots in Indochina and, through an OSS detachment, supplied intelligence on Japanese and Vichy French troop movements. All this, he had hoped, would curry favor with the US government and generate sympathy for the anti-French rebellion. He even sent a letter to President Franklin Roosevelt beseeching his support. However, Ho Chi Minh had miscalculated America's growing mistrust of all things Communist.

Casting their lot with the French, America responded by sending a Military Assistance and Advisory Group (MAAG) to Vietnam in 1950. MAAG was the command group responsible for all US military advisors in foreign countries. The MAAG in Vietnam was to supervise the millions of dollars in US equipment being used by the French. By 1953, however, it was clear that the French were losing ground to the Viet Minh.

After the French were defeated at Dien Bien Phu the following year, negotiations at the Geneva Conference separated Vietnam into two political entities: a northern zone, governed by the Communist Viet Minh, and a southern zone, which became the Republic of Vietnam.

In 1955, after Vanderpool validated his battalion's training, thus certifying them ready for any potential deployment, he received orders to Fort Rucker, Alabama—"where they were opening the Army Aviation School." The assignment was no doubt a surprise, as Jay was not an aviator. As an artilleryman, he was familiar with the liaison role of coordinating close air support, and how to act as an aerial spotter for adjusting indirect fires. But beyond these liaison roles, his knowledge of Army Aviation was fundamental at best.

To complicate matters further, "Army Aviation" was still trying to establish its identity and purpose. One lingering question was:

Should the Army have fixed-wing assets?

And if so, what would these aviation assets do?

Apart from the latter-day Army Air Forces, "Army Aviation" traced its immediate lineage to a small cadre of fixed-wing aircraft belonging to the Army Ground Forces. These planes (including Piper L-4 Grasshoppers and Stinson L-5 Sentinels) were largely relegated to fire support roles—adjusting artillery and naval gunfire, or conducting aerial reconnaissance. Most of the pilots and ground crews received their initial training via the Department of Air Training at the Field Artillery School at Fort Sill, although some were trained through the Army Air Forces pipeline. After 1947, when the US Air Force became its own separate service, the Army continued developing its own fixed-wing and rotary aircraft units to support its ground operations.

At the time of Vanderpool's arrival, the Army Aviation School had just begun its transition from Fort Sill to Fort Rucker. "They were developing a force of troops, an infantry regiment, an artillery battalion, and an engineer company, to provide troops for school training [and] for tactical training."

At first, Jay thought his assignment would fulfill nothing more than an administrative training role. "A little later," however, "the commanding general, General Carl Hutton asked me to take over a project, then ongoing, of arming fixed-wing, Army-type aircraft to be tested in the anti-tank role, Project ABLE BUSTER." This tasking officially made Jay Vanderpool the Chief of the Combat Development Office at Fort Rucker.

"For that," he said, "we were selecting various types of light aircraft . . . and assorted weapons: rockets, machine guns, and napalm bombs. We didn't have missiles at that time. We completed that test and studies and made a report. It went to Washington [and] died on the vine in the inter-service rivalry debate between the Army and Air Force." Despite their common ancestry, the Army and Air Force were arguing over whether the former should have fixed-wing, close air support assets.

Hutton, disappointed that the Air Force was giving him so much bureaucratic grief, called Jay into his office with a pointed question.

"Do you think we could make a fighting helicopter?"

Hutton knew that the Army's fixed-wing aircraft concept was going to die in the Pentagon. Thus, he asked Vanderpool if there was any viability in arming the new-fangled helicopter.

"Well," Jay replied, "we could arm it. I don't know whether it will work or not, but we could arm it and find out."

To that point, the Army had done some initial experiments with mockups, static tests, and gunsight cameras. "The camera work indicated to most observers," said Jay, "that the helicopter was too unstable a platform for launching current weapons."

These same critics, however, conceded that the helicopter's role as a utility aircraft (as demonstrated in Korea) was its true forte. In fact, the Korean War had validated the growing versatility of helicopters to perform missions not covered by the Air Force. The mountainous terrain, combined with the enemy's strength in numbers, had put the Americans at a disadvantage in terms of mobility. These disadvantages, however, were partially offset by the near-impromptu introduction of tactical helicopters. As Lieutenant General John Tolson recalled: "Many thoughtful officers had watched the little observation helicopter-turned-ambulance flit up and down the steep hills with effortless agility. It was not hard to envision the possibilities inherent in hundreds of larger machines carrying combat troops up and over those deadly slopes."

After Korea, a few senior leaders revisited their studies of the lessons learned, comparing campaign data against "hypothetical airmobile operations under the same conditions." Almost simultaneously, in April 1954, Major General James M. Gavin, an airborne pioneer from World War II, published an article in *Harper's Magazine* titled "Cavalry, and I Don't Mean Horses!" wherein he envisioned using the helicopter as a means to achieve vertical envelopment. The concept of vertical envelopment harkened back to the days of World War II, when parachute infantry would descend onto the enemy from the third dimension. Using helicopters, however, could achieve similar effects but with quicker results . . . and with a lower logistical burden.

During those gestational years of the mid-1950s, Gavin sought inroads with the Army School System. With Fort Benning as their initial starting point, the Army created an Airmobility Division to develop the doctrines, tactics, and organizational concepts for helicopter warfare. These early efforts at Fort Benning, however, focused primarily on using the helicopter as a "battlefield taxi"—a means to deliver troops to the frontlines in a manner similar to the parachute infantry over Europe and the Pacific. These sentiments were echoed in the new field manual FM 57-35: *Army Transport Aviation-Combat Operations*. "The basic tactics and techniques described in this manual stood the test of time," said General Tolson, "and would be vindicated in the tests of the 11th Air Assault Division [later rebranded as the 1st Cavalry Division] and in Vietnam."

Comparatively little attention, however, had been given using the helicopter as a mobile weapons platform similar to the fixed-wing close air support platforms. The offices at Fort Benning did, however, develop plans for a "lightweight, simple, flexible turret gun to be provided for all Army transport helicopters."

But the turret gun was never developed as conceived.

From their offices at Fort Rucker, however, Hutton and Vanderpool hoped to find a way to make the "armed helicopter" a reality.

"We selected the Bell H-13 helicopter as our basic mount," said Jay. The H-13s were among the most versatile in the Aviation School fleet. Manufactured by Bell Aircraft, the H-13 had seen extensive service during the Korean War, mostly as an observation and medevac aircraft. "Also, the cross-tubing on the skids was an easy place for our blacksmiths to tie weapons to," Jay continued. "We had maintenance backup. We also believed if we could effectively shoot from the H-3, we could certainly do it from bigger, more powerful aircraft. So, we took the smallest machine available, and gave it a full test with the maximum load. To do this, we had a team of just five people; myself, two officers and two enlisted men. We had no machine shop's support for it, except the post shop. We did our own manufacturing; we cut and pasted, hammered, beat and ironed until all hours. We worked around the clock, every night until twelve, one, two o'clock in the morning, and up in the morning and at it again."

Two weeks later, Vanderpool and his team emerged from the workshop with a highly-modified, highly-armed H-13. "On the first ship we tested, the first package [consisted of] two 50 caliber aerial machine guns from World War II. The machine gun had a heavy recoil, which we softened with an Edgewater Adapter. Though, in thinking it over . . . I was worried about whether the recoil of the machine guns would tear the helicopter apart. What would the reverse thrust do when you fire those machine guns forward? What would the reverse thrust do to the angle of attack? We could have started with a 30, but we knew that if [the helicopter] could handle a 50 without tearing or shaking the machine apart, [it] could handle the 30."

Luckily, the 50-cal machine gun fired without compromising the airframe.

"We got some gun sights from the Navy; also firing devices, intervalometers, etc. . . . and wired them to the system. Now, the reason we could do this was because of Captain Harold Hennington, who was my project engineer . . . or rather, he called himself the project blacksmith. He had been a B-25 pilot in World War II and had fired a lot of machine guns, rockets . . . and was familiar with the weaponry that we had available. Harold was given the job of tying it together."

Because Harold was a fixed-wing pilot, however, Vanderpool's group turned to Captain Monty Montgomery, one of the Army's top rotary-wing instructor pilots. "We picked him for two reasons," Jay recalled. "One he's a damn good pilot; secondly, he didn't weigh very much. We knew this package [the fully-loaded H-13] was going to be pretty heavy, and we didn't want a big heavy man adding to the weight load." The two enlisted men who rounded out the group were selected for their expertise in administrative matters and helicopter maintenance.

"We didn't have any particular desire to join Billy Mitchell," Jay quipped—referring to Mitchell's infamous court martial of 1925. "We had no authority, no money, nothing but the guts of the brigadier general Army aviator, Carl Hutton."

It was, by all accounts, an independent project.

"By word of mouth, some people knew we were going to try it. We didn't tell anyone in writing; we weren't that silly." Around Fort Rucker, though, Vanderpool and his associates (Hennington, Montgomery, and their two enlisted aides) took on the reluctant nickname "Vanderpool's Fools," as many thought they were crazy for trying to mount conventional weapons to helicopters.

Satisfied that the H-13 could withstand the wear-and-tear of machine gun fire, Vanderpool went shopping for a suitable rocket launcher. The problem, however, was that none of the current American-built rockets were designed for zero-launch speeds. "Those that were available were designed to be launched from tubes," he said, "but their accuracy was not very good."

But Jay found a lifeline, of sorts, in the Oerlikon 8-centimeter aerial rocket.

"It looked the best on dispersion."

The Oerlikon had typically been affixed to combat aircraft with operational speeds in excess of 140 knots. "I observed that Oerlikon set on a very short travel rail," Jay continued, "about a couple of inches... held by a twelve-G shear pin as a safety for hard landings. Now I analyzed the ignition rate on the motor. We found that within about a few milliseconds, that rocket was in full thrust. What I was hoping for was that the 12-G shear pin would hold the rocket on long enough to build up flying thrust and when it came off it wouldn't tumble and blow up under our nose."

Having independently tested the machine guns and rockets, Vanderpool's team went out to Matteson Range (as it would later be called) for a combined static test on the helicopter. "We built a wooden platform about four or five feet high. We strapped the ship down, so if something went wrong, it wouldn't blow away." They fired the machine guns in successively-increasing bursts, firing as many as 20–30 rounds per gun . . . with no structural damage to the helicopter.

"It seemed to be working."

Next was the rocket-firing test.

"We fired a single rocket down range," he said. "Surprisingly, coming off that zero-length rail launch . . . it went straight down range and a little bit short of the aiming point. We fired a couple more. Then we fired a ripple of four; all of them were going down range. We had much greater accuracy, much greater than we'd ever hoped for."

But now, Vanderpool wanted to test the rocket's trajectory under different variables.

Could the rocket maintain its accuracy under simulated combat conditions?

To find out, Jay ordered Montgomery to crank up another helicopter, and hover it over the static-mounted helicopter while pulling a downward pitch. With this maneuver, Vanderpool was hoping to place some rotor wash over the weapons.

"The down-wash was to test the effect on the rocket," he said.

He wanted to see if the heat and turbulence from the rotor wash would skew the rocket's trajectory. But after firing a single rocket (followed by a four-rocket volley, fired at 100 millisecond intervals), Jay was relieved to see the rockets meet their target with near-pinpoint accuracy.

"It got them off like a spitball coming out of a tube," he beamed.

Now it was time to test the rocket's trajectory from a hovering platform.

"We told Monty not to get more than about two or three hundred feet," said Jay, "because if he fell, we wanted to be able to find the pieces."

Taking the fully-loaded H-13 into the air, Montgomery settled his aircraft into a steady hover just above two-hundred feet. As expected, he fired the machine guns without incident. But the team collectively held their breath as Monty prepared to fire his rockets. The baited breaths soon turned to relief as three rockets emerged from the H-13 . . . all with great accuracy and no disruption to the helicopter's in-flight performance. "Then off he took and circled around, which he wanted to do all the time," Jay recalled. "You know he felt like a dive bomber pilot by that time. He took the ship around and fired in flight right near us so we could watch him."

Montgomery fired an additional three volleys before coming back to land.

During the immediate post-flight inspection (assisted by Bell Helicopter engineers), Jay beamed that: "We couldn't find any material damage. We had proven a point that had never been proven to our knowledge." They had just proven the viability of using the helicopter as a close air support weapon.

But proving its viability was only the first step.

Now, Vanderpool had to devise a way to employ the helicopter effectively.

Immediately following the hovering live-fire test, General Hutton approached Jay and said: "Van, I want you to come up with a company-sized air cavalry organization; determine the aircraft requirements; draw up an organizational sketch; and draw up a maneuver plan. Get the people from the Assistant Commandant, and on Sunday morning we will have a parade ground look at the organization. Sunday afternoon, we will have a maneuver."

Per Hutton's orders, Jay Vanderpool now had to develop an entire organizational structure and its tactical doctrines in less than 36 hours.

"We were compressing our R&D into tactics pretty quickly," he said bluntly. "That Friday night, I drew up the first air cavalry concept, sitting at my dining room table." Although an artilleryman by trade, he had a wealth of practical experience in cavalry/recon operations—from his childhood hobbies of hunting & trapping, to his military expeditions through the Pacific War. Still, he needed a solid base upon which to create a written body of tactics.

To that end, he drew lessons from the Napoleonic Wars.

"I relied, as most people do, on basic things," he said. "I was thinking of some European experience." In studying the battles of Napoleon and the Duke of Wellington, Vanderpool drew distinctions between two types of cavalry soldiers—those who fought and reconnoitered exclusively on horseback; and those who rode to the battlefield on horseback, but then *dismounted* to fight (i.e., dragoons). Both were supported by rapid-deployment artillery, and all elements were controlled by a tactical command headquarters. With that organizational concept in mind, Vanderpool envisioned an "air cavalry" team wherein the latter-day mounted horsemen would become the recon and gunship pilots; the dragoons would become the airmobile infantrymen; and the supporting artillery would have its own spotters within its own helicopters.

"That's what I drew and sketched out," he said.

"I sketched it based on the available aircraft."

Jay decided that they would start with a platoon of attack helicopters, H-13s, in the cavalry role. "We would need a platoon of infantry [the airmobile "dragoons"], then would put in a base of fire with some gunships . . . the H-19, because we knew we had them in our inventory, and some supply and evacuation ships."

By Sunday morning, pilot instructors—civilian and military—from all across Fort Rucker had arrived for the experimental maneuvers. "Most of these civilians had had either Air Force, Navy, Army, or other military training before they were instructor pilots at Fort Rucker," said Vanderpool. "They were as well-trained or better-trained, probably, on military concepts than some of the young pilots we had. I explained the concept to them, briefed them, then went through the process . . . to pick out who would be the first ones."

After lunch, Vanderpool hoarded the first round of pilots into their helicopters. Based on two hours of briefing, the test pilots validated every tactical task—including employment of the reconnaissance assets, delivering airmobile troops, bringing up the base of fire, delivering logistical support, and providing casualty evacuations. "It was the standard Wellington ideas from Europe," he said, "Duke of Wellington ideas that had been tested and re-tested. The only thing that changed was the helicopter for the horse."

For the next several weeks, "Vanderpool's Fools" tested hardware during the week and maneuvered on weekends. "We tested the available machine guns, which at the time were primarily the aerial 30 and 50-caliber on different aircraft." Aside from their inaugural H-13 helicopter, Vanderpool and his men evaluated the H-23, H-19, H-25, H-21, and H-34. "We also tested available rockets on all the same aircraft to see what could or could not be done," he added. "Concurrently, we were out trying to find if there were other weapons that might be better than the World War II weapons we had available."

To that end, Vanderpool enlisted help from the Army ordnance arsenals. "They started looking around, helping us, and if they found something, they gave me a call," he said. "I'd fly out and take a look at it, scrounge it, or try to get it and bring it home. We would bring home a few thousand rockets or whatever weapons we could find."

By the fall of 1956, Vanderpool had secured authorization to create a test platoon. "A platoon gave us more blacksmiths," he said. "Each pilot and his enlisted assistant were responsible for arming their own ship." Indeed, Jay would give them a helicopter, a handful of machine guns and rocket launchers, and say: "This is yours, go to it."

But, as Vanderpool admitted, this impromptu modification process was chaotic. "The pilots were not trained machinists, but they were all pretty good blacksmiths." Together, every pilot and his enlisted aide were cutting metal and bolting hardware. They wired and hung various pieces of ordnance together to make a combat-effective helicopter. But although these "Frankenstein" helicopters had the necessary equipment, Vanderpool and his men had to start "demonstrating weapons and tactics in order to sell the concept."

Even though helicopters were understood to be the Army's domain, Jay knew that the air cavalry ideas would come under fire from interservice rivalries. "If it was presented philosophically to the Pentagon," he said, "we knew we'd never get anywhere . . . it would take us 30 years." Practical demonstrations would be the only way to quell the perennial nay-sayers within the Pentagon. Even still, the Army at large remained skeptical about the air cavalry concept—"in fact, a lot of Army aviators were not convinced."

But Jay found that the receptiveness to air cavalry differed among the services.

"We found at the lower levels, the Air Force and Navy understood it better than the Army people did. They were fighter/bomber people and [they] knew what we were trying to do, and some of them had gone through the same developments during World War II."

Throughout 1956, "Vanderpool's Fools" took their helicopter demonstration team on tour. They would fly mock maneuvers at any military installation that would host them. Whenever Vanderpool and his men couldn't get an invite, they simply hosted their own invitational events at Fort Rucker. Their biggest break, however, came with the Association of the United States Army (AUSA) symposium, which was held at Fort Rucker that year. "At that time, we showed it to captains of industry [including some of the biggest defense contractors] and a number of senior military leaders—including some Air Force generals from the Air War College. The latter were not as enthusiastic as we were."

Among the high-ranking attendees was General Willard Wyman of Continental Army Command (CONARC). CONARC was the largest of the Army's commands and was responsible for maintaining the readiness of the Army's operational field forces. It was the forerunner to the modern-day Forces Command (FORSCOM). Also in attendance were several officers from the Army's Research & Development (R&D) labs, and a slew of Army aviators from the Operations Staff at the Pentagon.

"For the Army, we had primarily people who had a direct personal interest to see if the program was going to go." In fact, one of the senior leaders who had sent his representatives from R&D was Lieutenant General Gavin, the same paratrooper who had forecasted the heliborne cavalry concept in his 1954 article for *Harper's Magazine*. "At the unveiling everything went quite well," Jay recalled. "We were able to partially convince quite a few people."

By 1957, Jay had expanded the demonstration itinerary to Fort Benning, Fort Knox, Fort Bliss, White Sands Missile Range, and Redstone. "Anytime we got a captive audience, we'd show air cavalry to them. You know how the schools like to entertain from time to time. They like to bring in outside interests to add color to their own program."

While managing the air cavalry roadshow, Jay spent much of 1957–58 refining the tactics and doctrines for the heliborne concept. "We'd maneuver on our range or other Army post ranges. We encouraged two-sided maneuvers with ground troops versus airmobile troops. We let each commander use whatever ingenuity he had to see if the concept would work, or if he could find a weak point in it." Vanderpool knew that their input was critical to making the airmobile concept work. "During those early days, I had written all of the tactical doctrine and concepts personally. This becomes a chore when you have a lot of other things to do. I was writing all the concept work on a kitchen table at night"—and there were very few people at Fort Rucker who could give Jay's tactics and concepts a "reality check" from an infantryman's perspective.

Meanwhile, General Hutton had taken another command in Europe, and was replaced at Fort Rucker by General Bogardus "Bugs" Cairns. A 1932 West Point graduate, Cairns had distinguished himself in combat during the Battle of Kasserine Pass, successfully repelling a German assault while leading Combat Command B of the 1st Armored Division. "Cairns was a cavalry officer," said Vanderpool—a cavalryman who had spent his formative years in the horse-mounted regiments of the prewar Army. "Somewhere in his footlockers," Jay continued, "he found the old 1936 yellowback cavalry manual."

"Can you use this?" asked Cairns.

"It was perfect," said Jay.

Indeed, Cairns' twenty-year-old manual depicted the baseline tactics and terminology needed to sell "air cavalry" to the institutional Army. "We knew what we wanted to do," Jay later said, "but when we put it into words that old cavalrymen could understand, it would be more convincing. We took that 1936 yellowback cavalry manual and . . . took the horse cavalry portion of it and substituted helicopters for horses, using the same language and terminology."

As a result, the air cavalry concept finally had a receptive audience.

"Older soldiers—I mean two, three, and four-star generals—could understand the language of their day [the late 1930s]. It did help sell the concept." Retooling the 1936 manual into an air cavalry guidebook, Vanderpool printed nearly 200 copies and "sent it all over the United States to any US Army School that would accept it."

His efforts were well-received.

"Our training text was adopted almost in its entirety to become the first tactical doctrine of air cavalry/sky cavalry/airmobile [warfare]. The weaponry progressed as we tested everything available in the arsenal."

One shortcoming that Vanderpool noticed within the US arsenal, however, was the lack of a guided missile. In fact, the Army had just cancelled development of their own prototype SSM-A-23 Dart guided missile, and began shopping for a foreign-built stopgap solution.

Coincidentally, the French Army had just fielded the SS.10 wire-guided, anti-tank missile to its frontline forces. "We sent a team of four or five people over to France [in 1958]," Jay recalled, "to study the French wire guided system." The SS.10 had been developed by Lieutenant Colonel Jean Bastien-Thiry, a French Air Force officer and weapons engineer.[16] Development began in 1948, when the French munitions company *Arsenal de l'Aéronautique* was evaluating further development of the latter-day German X-7 missile.

The US Army had previously evaluated the prototype SS.10 in 1952–53, but concluded that the missile needed further development for viable field use. During the interim, however, the French

Army successfully delivered more than thirty SS.10s to the Israeli Defense Forces in 1955. And, in the wake of the SSM-A-23's cancellation, an American team arrived in France to reevaluate the operational SS.10. "The French were, at that time, trying SS.10s and SS.11s on the Allouette [helicopter]," said Vanderpool. "Our people went to the ground school there, to learn how to hook it up, how to guide it, and how to operate it. When they came back, they were able to use the missile."

As such, in February 1959, the US Army adopted the SS.10. "We hooked them to the sides of our H-13s and we had our anti-tank weapons," he said. "They were pretty good up to 1,200 meters . . . getting about a three-point kill, which is not too bad for that stage of development." But the SS.10 and SS.11 were still stopgaps—intended for temporary use until the Army developed its own replacements. By 1963, the SS.10/11-series had been phased out in favor of the MGM-21A.

But for Jay Vanderpool, the greater victory was giving his H-13 helicopter the capacity to kill a tank. "Of course, exposure time for the pilot was a lot longer than we wanted." But as Jay conceded: "We weren't looking for the ultimate weapon; we were looking for concepts. The French wire-guided missile proved to us that the concept was feasible and could be applied to our helicopters."

All the while, Jay Vanderpool had a unique status as both an "official" and "unofficial" Army aviator. When he initially assumed his role as the chief of Fort Rucker's Combat Developments Office, Jay and his commanders knew that, in order to keep the "armed helicopter" concept alive, they couldn't assign it to only one project officer. "We decided also the best home for the concept would probably be in Combat Developments, who could provide a home for it for years as necessary."

Part of his weekly duties within the Combat Developments Office included flying as an "observer" aboard various helicopters—"10 to 20 hours per week." Given that proximity, General Cairns wanted to put Vanderpool through an impromptu flight school, and get him ready for a solo flight. "I'm going to try to get you through, and make you an Army aviator," said Cairns. "Get ready to solo, then I'll go to work on it."

Vanderpool was up to the task, but Cairns had to navigate a complex and mercurial bureaucracy that often stonewalled elder officers trying to earn an "aviator" status. As such, even with Vanderpool's check flights and ratings, it would be a difficult task to get him branded as an "aviator."

Said Jay of his flight training: "I went out and like everyone, I eventually learned to hover, then learned to fly, then learned to do my auto rotations to the ground." After completing twenty auto rotations and nearly 150 flight hours—"which is more than most students get"—Vanderpool was considered ready to fly. "In fact, all my grades had been awarded," he said. "These warrant officer instructor pilots would test me and they would give me the lowest possible grade they could to pass me. In case I wrecked the airplane, they didn't want to be responsible," he laughed.

"After all the check rides . . . all I had to do was get permission and put on my wings. Well, there was a lot of politicking going on in the Army, like there always is, in all organizations . . . and many people didn't want any more colonels coming into the program and knocking out jobs for the younger flying officers. I was blocked at least temporarily at that time. General Cairns pulled some deal [perhaps through CONARC or the Department of Army Aviation]. They put me on flight status and I drew full flight pay, and I could fly anywhere I wanted to, but I always had to have a co-pilot with me, until I officially soloed."

Even with publication of the revamped 1936 manual (and his grand reception at Fort Rucker's AUSA Symposium), Vanderpool still had to contend with skeptics among the various Army posts. One flashpoint of skepticism occurred during his team's visit to Fort Bliss, Texas. "I was given a mission to write a script for an Air Cavalry demonstration at Fort Bliss," he recalled. "It was in the summertime," wherein the dry heat and the subsequent air density at lower altitudes would impact flight operations. By the same token, however, Vanderpool knew how to use the desert conditions to his advantage.

"I wrote a script which, in essence, was tied to a desert terrain that I knew; I had been raised in the desert country," he said. "I knew from having lost a lot of cows out in the prairie, it may look perfectly flat, but you can easily lose a herd of 20 or 30 cows . . . they're down in those swales. On the bottom of each little swale is a little fringe of brush, where roots get through, to get some moisture out of the gravel. These brushlines, from low altitude or even up a few thousand feet, very distinctly point out the wet weather stream line. Taking advantage of this knowledge of desert terrain and vegetation, I wrote a scenario in which I compared the helicopter to the jackrabbit. In El Paso, people would understand the analogy. The jackrabbit, when running, would jump way up in the air and look around, then drop back out of sight, and run some more. I decided I would run the helicopters on the same concept."

As it turned out, the scripted event was once again part of an AUSA gathering—this time for a "missile symposium at Fort Bliss," he added, "because there is a missile school there." Indeed, Fort Bliss was the proverbial "home" of the US Army's Air Defense Artillery Corps. Just across the Texas border, in New Mexico, lay White Sands Missile Range, the veritable proving ground for America's growing arsenal of tactical missiles.

For the event, Vanderpool placed his reconnaissance helicopters two to three miles out from their objective, while telling the spectators about his rabbit analogy.

"Well, it worked even better than I expected."

The pilots, having studied the terrain during their numerous rehearsal flights, could clearly see the vegetation streamlines. "I picked, as our objective, an area where several of these streamlines converged," said Jay. "We established a hypothetical objective out there, in front of a bleacher where spectators would see this assault. We deployed the cavalry [helicopters] way off on the flank, two or three miles. We put the troop ships around behind us, where the spectators couldn't see them, back behind a hill, with the heavy gunships carrying a maximum load of rockets."

From the bleachers, the spectators could see reconnaissance helicopters off in the distance. "We put them all up, way out there on the horizon. They looked like little flies to us. You could just barely see them out there across the desert. It was a clear, bright day, not a cloud in the sky. This group of civilian and military spectators were sitting on the bleachers 10 or 15 feet above the ground."

Then, on cue, the H-13 gunships emerged from the swales. "Once in a while, you'd see a flicker of light cutting as the rotor blade would cut the line of view. You didn't see those rascals." But the first thing the spectators *clearly* saw that day, "was when the [H-13] choppers popped out of that desert, out of nowhere, and were already firing when they came into view." The audience sat in stunned silence as a chorus of H-13s and H-19s fired off their volleys of rockets. The awestruck observations continued as the airmobile troops landed, and the medical choppers conducted their evac demonstrations. As the last helicopter depopulated from the airspace, Vanderpool looked out among the spectators.

"There was not one word said; not one person spoke."

At first, he took it as a bad omen.

"Oh my God, what have we done wrong now?" he thought.

Finally, General Wyman from CONARC broke the awkward silence. He turned to General Maxwell Taylor, the Army Chief of Staff and said:

"Max, *that's* what I've been trying to tell you."

"I understand it now," Taylor replied. "I understand it."

To this point, "Vanderpool's Fools" had had support from CONARC, the ordnance arsenals, and the special interest groups within the aviation community. "Now, we had the Chief of Staff of the Army behind us," Jay beamed. "From then on, we were on the higher political pastures."

The scenario at Fort Bliss had been the perfect storm of luck and opportunity converging with hard work and preparation. "We didn't pick the terrain," said Jay, "we inherited the terrain, but the low altitude approach was what we had started with initially." Earlier, when Vanderpool and his comrades had been testing fixed-wing aircraft for anti-tank roles, they drew lessons from the USAAF's experience during the Pacific War—"when B-25s were employed out in the islands." During these bombing runs, Vanderpool noted that the B-25s had used "low altitude to get through the Japanese troops and anti-aircraft radar." Now with helicopters, Vanderpool wanted to make low-altitude flights a standard procedure for dodging radar. "Secondly, your exposure time to ground fire is much less if you're dodging between the trees, or just above the trees, at a given speed." Thus, from his earliest test flights at Fort Rucker, Vanderpool stressed the need to fly just above the tree canopy, or amongst the trees if possible. "And that became known as the 'nap of the earth,' [flying 'near as possible' to the earth] . . . that you could come down and sneak in between the existing accidents of terrain and whatever concealment might or might not be there." And the intervisibility swales of the El Paso desert had provided the perfect showcase for "nap of the earth" flying.

Humorously, the morning after Jay's demonstration at Fort Bliss, he noted that "the missile people were upset." As it turned out, the air cavalry demonstration had made the front page of the El Paso newspapers. As Jay recalled, the El Paso news media had become rather blasé about missiles.

"The reporters saw them every day."

By now, these missile demonstrations had become routine.

But: "They had never seen armed helicopters before."

Impressed by the agility and mobility of the Army's new rotor-craft, the morning papers eagerly headlined the air cavalry demo, relegating the missile symposium to a Page 3 story. "This made the air defense people very unhappy because it [the AUSA missile symposium] was their show," said Vanderpool. "AUSA had put up the money for it, but we got the major credit lines."

Perhaps in an effort to be fair, the afternoon edition papers reversed the story placement: "They put missiles on Page 1, and helicopters on Page 3," he recalled. But the air defense community still felt the sting. Intra-service rivalries and comparative publicity aside, Jay Vanderpool was elated that "we had made our point where we wanted it, which was to the senior officers of the Army." Now that the top brass had seen the concept in action, it would only be a matter of time before air cavalry came to fruition.

"Later, we conducted tests at Fort Knox," Jay recalled, whereupon his air cavalry pilots had perhaps the most unusual experience of their roadshow careers. During one maneuver involving inert

SS-10 air-to-ground missiles, Jay's pilots squared off against a platoon of tanks. Fort Knox was, at the time, home to the US Army's Armor School. "They came chugging out there in those tanks buttoned up. We made sure everything was buttoned [all tank hatches closed]," as a safety precaution, even though his pilots were firing inert warheads. "We had the chopper open up with four SS-10 missiles. He got two direct hits on a tank . . . which was better than our average. The Fort Knox people called the maneuver off immediately. They said it really was noisy inside those tanks, even with inert warheads. They even checked to confirm that our warheads were in fact inert."

Reflecting on his time as the Chief of Combat Developments in Fort Rucker, Vanderpool characterized his job as a mix of weapons development *and* doctrinal development. "The ordnance arsenal people were starting to get a little money for the program," he said, "so I worked with them quite a bit on conceptual development of weapons that might be applied later down the road." He also spent considerable time working with representatives from Bell Helicopters, Hiller Aircraft, and Sikorsky—developing concepts, optimizing aircraft designs, and addressing issues with the onboard powertrains. His job in developing an armed helicopter force was, in many respects, "policy-level" work—coordinating efforts among the various arsenals, CONARC personnel, and Pentagon staff to support the air cavalry concept. "That was my primary work at that period," he said, "trying to find more and more financial help and moral support. Before, we had moral support, but no money." But now, in the wake of the Fort Bliss demonstration, "we were getting some money plus *moral* support."

Almost simultaneously, the Army Aviation School began development of the ARMAIR Brigade concept. "We used a brigade-sized unit to develop conceptually the organizational, tactical, and doctrinal theories of airmobile forces employing helicopters in lieu of ground vehicles," said Vanderpool. In theory, ARMAIR was a virtual extension of the "sky cavalry" concepts that Jay had published earlier. Under ARMAIR, the heliborne cavalry elements were subordinate to a brigade headquarters and "provided for a completely airmobile combined arms unit with a capability for sustained operations." In turn, the brigade would provide a "high degree of mobility" while facilitating the commander's freedom of maneuver.

The brigade's organic helicopters, in their various roles, would provide "surveillance information, reconnaissance, and battlefield observation to all echelons of command." At the same time, helicopters could provide rapid direct-fire support. Moreover, ARMAIR increased the light infantry's overall speed by tethering it to the horsepower of the helicopter, "and not the pace of the foot soldier."

Still, the ARMAIR Brigade concept study didn't ignore the potential liabilities of airmobile operations. Operational advantages such as "faster reaction time, flexibility, high mobility, and direct fire support" could be offset by some inherent vulnerabilities—including exposure to ground fire; the cost of maintaining and transporting helicopter fleets; and the potential impact of adverse weather conditions. "A troop test and evaluation was proposed to study these problems." Those troop tests and evaluations would later take place under the auspices of the Howze Board during the early 1960s, the final stepping stone to creating a permanent airmobile force within the US Army.

"We printed hundreds of copies of the ARMAIR Brigade concept study," said Jay. "We saturated the Army combat development system. Everyone concerned had the same sheet of music. Our people lectured at all the other Army schools and study groups.

The ARMAIR Brigade study was the most widely-distributed Army aviation concept study produced prior to the Howze Board plan." In fact, when the Howze Board commenced operations at Fort Bragg, North Carolina, Vanderpool recalled that each of the principal members had copies of the ARMAIR Brigade study.

By 1959, Jay Vanderpool had spent four years toiling in the aviation shops at Fort Rucker. And, by virtue of the Army's mandated career metrics, it was time for a transfer. "I was then ordered to Headquarters, Seventh Army in Germany." It would be his first time serving along the Iron Curtain, the foremost "Frontier of Democracy" in the ongoing Cold War.

"While I was in Germany," he continued, "the people at Fort Rucker and Fort Benning continued their demonstrations." Although Jay never saw the final airmobile exercise, he heard that it was one of the most effective demonstrations of helicopter warfare to that date. Indeed, these demonstrations would ultimately facilitate the creation of the inaugural air cavalry division at Fort Benning, Georgia in 1964.

But for now, Jay Vanderpool was on his way to the Iron Curtain.

8

The Winter Soldier

Having spent his entire World War II career in the Pacific, Jay Vanderpool had only seen the European theater through various photographs and news reports. Although the Allied Occupation had formally ended in 1949, the realities of post-war Germany were hard to ignore. The country had been partitioned along ideological lines: East Germany was now a Communist state; West Germany was a fragile, ailing democracy. Throughout the late 1940s (and into the 1950s), the economies of both nations were in shambles—millions were starving, millions more were homeless, and several had taken to a life of crime. In fact, the emerging black market seemed to provide the only viable means of income.

During those inaugural years of the occupation, the Germans were collectively devastated by their nation's defeat. The seemingly-invincible *Wehrmacht* had been trounced, and Adolf Hitler's promise of a "Thousand-Year Reich" had ended, literally, in ruins. Meanwhile, the Allied Occupation followed a policy known as the "3 D's"—demilitarization, deindustrialization, and de-Nazification.

By the late-1950s, however, West Germany had been emerging from the post-World War II malaise. Understandably, Germans on both sides of the Iron Curtain were still embittered by their defeat. But under the banners of capitalism and democracy, the quality of life in West Germany was on the rise. East Germany, on the other hand, was falling farther into the abyss of Communism. At times, it seemed that the new East German state rivaled the tyranny of Hitler's Third Reich. Although life was comparatively better in the Federal Republic of Germany, the local citizens nevertheless resented the American presence in their homeland. After the fall of Nazi Germany, the US had established permanent bases throughout the West German countryside. These bases, known as "kasernes," were groupings of troop barracks situated near German towns including Frankfurt, Baumholder, Stuttgart, and Bad Kreuznach. Since the start of the Cold War, armored and mechanized units were stationed within these kasernes preparing for an anticipated showdown with the Eastern Bloc.

From what Jay Vanderpool could see, however, the European contingent was in bad shape. President Eisenhower had shifted America's combat stance to one of nuclear deterrence. Strategic retaliation was the rule of the day, and there was some speculation whether ground forces would remain relevant in the forthcoming "Nuclear Era." As a result, the US Army's training, readiness, and continuity of personnel suffered as more defense dollars were diverted to maintain the growing arsenal of strategic air and nuclear assets.

To make matters worse, there had been virtually no emphasis on training. By now, most of the training calendars throughout US Army Europe (USAEUR) had devolved into a cyclic routine of parades and sports competitions. Draconian defense budgets and toy soldier routines notwithstanding, however, the biggest problem for USAEUR was the political climate. Shortly after Jay's arrival in Germany, the Berlin Wall made its debut on the international stage. A formidable structure separating East from West, the Wall was referred to as the "Anti-Fascist Protection Rampart" by its

Communist constructors. The distinction was dubious, however, as it was simply a means to keep East Berliners away from the lures of capitalism. Meanwhile, Soviet Premier Nikita Khrushchev, never one for mild manners, had become openly more hostile towards the West. His provocative rhetoric at the United Nations, and his hardline stance at the 1961 Vienna Summit, hadn't won him any friends in the Free World.

Arriving at the Seventh Army Headquarters in Stuttgart, Jay reported to the G-4 section under Colonel Bill Strickland. "Why did you make me your logistics planner?" Jay asked. "I don't know much about logistics."

"I don't know much about logistics either," Strickland admitted.

Yet here he was the chief logistician for an entire field army.

"I'm the G-4," Strickland continued, "you might as well be the G-4 planner. Do it and learn it." From there, he gave Vanderpool barely two weeks to learn the dynamics of the job.

One of the things that caught Jay's foremost attention was the number of technical staff in the G-4—including warrant officers and civilians. "The technical people of course used to run everything except the major policy decisions and did a very fine job," he said. "I also got into the NATO logistics systems, which is interesting."

For example, the Spanish Army's artillery corps was still using the World War I-era British 75mm cannon. The problem, however, was that there were no replacement rounds for the British 75mm guns anywhere in the world. The Spaniards were literally holding the world's *last* reserve of 75mm ammunition for these World War I-era guns. Aside from this final store of ammunition, there were neither any replacement guns left in usable condition. Apart from these Spanish-operated artillery pieces, the only British 75s left in existence were museum pieces, or those on static display. Thus, to replenish the inevitable depletion of ammo, NATO planners would have to enlist a defense contractor to make new rounds according to the original specifications, or put more money down for a new artillery system.

"You ran into challenging problems in NATO logistics systems," said Jay, "but a lot of people . . . even at the national defense levels of the various countries were trying to see if they could come up with a common logistics system that NATO could use, that would simplify operations in case of an all-out war."

Easier said than done.

Every member of NATO had their own logistical system.

And those logistics were tied to public laws.

As Vanderpool recalled: "Someone appropriates the money to buy the beans and bullets, or petrol, or whatever it might be."

Thus, trying to integrate a system of logistics, across multiple countries, without having a common budgetary system, was next to impossible. "So, unless you have a common tax base," Vanderpool concluded, "it's going to be awfully hard to have a common logistics system." From his station at the G-4, Vanderpool saw how the various NATO partners tried to coordinate their logistics—including the West Germans, French, British, and Italians. "It was interesting to see," he said, "how the different people were solving similar problems."

To address the problem from USAEUR's end, Vanderpool described a concept known as the Mobile Army General Supply Point. "Had it been called a logistical task force," he added, "I could have understood the term better." Under the Mobile Army General Supply Point, a field army would "provide supplies for each division area or each corps area . . . which would reduce the line of communication from division back to the field army depot." The mobile supply point would operate under its own commander, a logistician of some stripe—"whether he was ordnance, quartermaster, or infantry, it wouldn't make any difference, but someone who understood logistics, supply and maintenance."

Vanderpool lauded the idea, but he wasn't surprised when the Pentagon shot it down. By the dawn of the 1960s, Jay recalled that the Pentagon was trying to dismantle the Army Technical Services (consisting of the Chemical Warfare Service; Corps of Engineers; Medical Department; Ordnance Department; Quartermaster Department; Signal Corps; and Transportation Department). "The Technical Services supported this task force concept," he said, "therefore it must be wrong." Dismissive parochialism aside, Jay thought that the Mobile Army General Supply Point was a good idea. "It was the first time I've ever seen all seven technical services try to cooperate to get a job done without worrying about their own particular service. However, it came at an unfortunate time in history, when their bosses back in the Pentagon were about to get fired anyway, and their service demoted. So, it never got off the ground."

Meanwhile, back in the States, President Kennedy took a fresh look at the airmobile concept. After Jay departed Fort Rucker, and during his few years in Europe, a strong tide of bureaucratic resentment had put air cavalry and air mobility on the backburner. However, in 1962, at the behest of Secretary of Defense Robert McNamara, the Army convened the Tactical Mobility Requirements Board at Fort Bragg. Headed by General Hamilton Howze, the board's mission was to test the viability of integrating helicopters into the Army's tactical formations. After some deliberation, the board recommended creating an airmobile "test" division equipped with 459 helicopters.

This new division would include airmobile infantry battalions and an air cavalry squadron to provide aerial reconnaissance and close air support. For the occasion, the Army reactivated the 11th Airborne Division in February 1963 and re-designated it the 11th Air Assault Division (Test).

The Howze Board, as it came to be known, "was authorized to pull in people from anywhere in the world they needed, or equipment they needed, to run the test as best they could in the time available," Jay recalled. Not coincidentally, Jay Vanderpool was among the many individuals tapped for temporary duty on the Howze Board. Given his role in formulating the initial air cavalry doctrines (as well as physically arming the helicopters), it came as no surprise when Jay was "ordered back from Germany to participate as a member of the board."

Other board members included Brigadier Generals Cliff Von Kann and Bogardus Cairns—both of whom were alumni of the Army's still-experimental program of putting senior officers through flight training. As Jay recalled: "A number of these senior officers had been aviators for one or two years. They were experienced in armor, infantry, artillery, or whatever their background might have been." Each of these latter-day aviators offered a critical perspective on how their parent branches operated. Consequently, their perspectives would reconcile the requirements of airmobility against the realities and limitations of their parent branches. Indeed, for an airmobile unit to be effective, it needed to fully synchronize its operations and capabilities with the basic branches that fed into it—particularly the infantry and artillery. "General Howze, of course, was an aviator and had been Chief of Army Aviation in the Pentagon earlier," Jay added. "When they pulled this team together, it was well weighted with knowledgeable, dedicated and convinced people."

As the 11th Air Assault Division came online, the Army selected General Harry WO Kinnard as the unit's inaugural commander. "It was ordered to Fort Benning and set up for training," said Vanderpool. Over the next two years, the 11th Air Assault Division would grow in manpower and equipment, testing and validating the concepts of helicopter warfare. "General Kinnard pulled together people from around the country and, again, staffing it quite a bit with these senior aviators who had gone through our training course at Fort Rucker."

By the end of 1964, the 11th Air Assault Division had conducted two massive field exercises in the Carolinas. Attended by senior Army leaders and defense planners, *Air Assault I* and *Air Assault II* demonstrated the multi-dimensional viability of helicopter warfare, and the 11th Air Assault Division was then fully integrated into the Army force structure.

Meanwhile, the situation in Vietnam had steadily gone from bad to worse. Per the Geneva Accords, the Republic of Vietnam was to hold a reunification election in 1956. However, Ngo Dinh Diem, the South Vietnamese President, cancelled the elections and vowed to stamp out any lingering Communists in the Republic of Vietnam. The Viet Minh operatives who remained in the south (the first incarnation of the Viet Cong) reciprocated by launching a low-level insurgency in 1957. After the French withdrew from Vietnam, MAAG stepped in to assist Diem in his anti-communist efforts.

By the fall of 1963, the Viet Cong insurgency had grown to a level that Washington could no longer ignore. Soon, MAAG would be dissolved into the newly-created Military Assistance Command, Vietnam (MACV)[2]—thereby giving the US a wider berth to send

---

[2] Pronounced "mack-vee."

conventional forces into Southeast Asia. Almost simultaneously, President Kennedy lost his confidence in Ngo Dinh Diem's ability to rule South Vietnam. On November 2, 1963, just weeks before Kennedy's own assassination, Ngo Dinh Diem was deposed and murdered in a coup d'état that was sanctioned, if not partially orchestrated by Washington.

With Diem now out of the way, the Hanoi government felt it was time to escalate the war and "liberate" South Vietnam. They felt that it wasn't enough to provide guns and ammunition to the Viet Cong. The time had come to intervene militarily with units of the People's Army of North Vietnam. They argued that these better-trained and highly motivated soldiers could infiltrate the south and make short work of the unmotivated South Vietnamese Army.

"I was [still] at Benning at the time [1963]," said Jay, "and we were trying to get something over there [to Vietnam] that could defeat the terrain and weather . . . the mud, rice paddies, and swamps over there. Vietnam appeared to be a good place to field test the Air Cavalry/Airmobile concept." Two years later, in the summer of 1965, the 11th Air Assault Division was officially re-designated as the 1st Cavalry Division (Airmobile).

But as Vietnam devolved further into chaos, Jay Vanderpool was recalled to his post with the Seventh Army in Europe. Although it was far away from the percolating conflict in Southeast Asia, Jay admitted that: "I learned an awful lot. We planned at all levels"—from battalion task force to Army Group. Coordinating logistics for the defense of Western Europe, however, put him at the mercy of the Pentagon's and the President's personal whims. Vanderpool recalled that whenever the White House or the Pentagon wanted to revise the defensive plans for Western Europe, they often wanted the revised plans the very next day.

"We worked a lot of nights," he said.

"But after a few years, we could crank up a pretty good and feasible plan in a few hours." Completing his tour in Europe, Jay Vanderpool returned stateside in 1964, whereupon he was assigned to the United States Strike Command at MacDill Air Force Base, Florida.

Strike Command was, in many ways, a forerunner to the modern-day US Central Command (CENTCOM). "I was again in logistics," he said, "where I learned quite a bit about transportation of people and things, because the Joint Task Forces and the Rapid Deployment Force always start with a movement." It was a nod to the old adage: "Equipment wins the battle; logistics wins the war." As Jay recalled: "From CONUS [the continental US], you must go somewhere to fight. You always start off with a movement problem"—sometimes accompanied by pre-stocked assets. "Then you have a tremendous line of communications behind you."

In fact, it was during his time with Strike Command that he saw how quickly a Joint Task Force could fail due to logistical problems.

"We had a flap down in the Congo," he recalled.

"It was decided to bring in some paras [paratroopers] from Belgium to the British-held Ascension Island. They were scheduled to be jumped into the Belgian Congo from American aircraft [C-130s], whereupon the Belgians would assume control under some vague chain of command. Of course, these operations had to be highly-classified. You don't tell everyone in town that it's going to happen."

But this operation was so highly-classified that no one had told Strike Command about it until the paratroopers were already in the air. The short notice was problematic for one reason:

There was no petrol station on the island to refuel the C-130s.

"We had airplanes in the air," said Jay, "but no way to refuel them."

Trying not to panic, Vanderpool and his team made a series of hurried phone calls to New York, London, Brussels, and other logistics centers, trying to find any oil tankers at sea that could be diverted to Ascension. "We found two or three tankers that were headed from somewhere in the Atlantic with the type of petrol we needed for these C-130s and other aircraft."

Jay then called Tactical Air Command (USAF) to release some of their reserve fuel tanks at Langley Air Force Base, Virginia. "The Air Force loaded up their collapsible rubber tanks and flew them to Ascension," he recalled. "We diverted those ships at sea, pulled them up to the beach, and started pumping [gas] into the rubber bladders." Although these diverted tankers were loaded with the requisite fuel, there was still the lingering problem of an idle C-130 on the runway of a British-held island. It would take nearly three days for the oil tankers to reach Ascension, even at full steam. This meant that the Pentagon would have to come up with a cover story, explaining to the British government why an American C-130 (carrying Belgian paratroopers) was sitting idly on its territorial runway. "Well, they came up with some kind of a cover story," said Jay, "that no one really believed, but the truth was we didn't have any gas and the planes couldn't go any further." But the ships finally arrived, and the fully-refueled C-130s made the final leg of their trip into the Congo.

When he wasn't fixing logistical nightmares, or coordinating emergency refuels, Jay spent most of his time coordinating efforts with the J-3 (Operations), planning various joint training exercises. "Concurrently, we worked with J-5 to plan [potential] combat operations in Africa, south of the Sahara and the Middle East. We normally conducted large joint tactical field exercises in the United States each year. The ground troops were provided by the Continental Army Command. The air equipment and people were produced by Tactical Air Command." Strike Command, meanwhile, provided the Joint Task Force commanders and the attendant staffs.

As Vanderpool described it: "These were large exercises involving 150–200,000 military people maneuvering across two or more states." Aside from the task force commander and staff teams, Strike Command also provided the scenarios, rules of engagement, and an observer-controller function to referee the unit's internal actions. "Those were probably the largest continental maneuvers since early World War II," he added. "They were comparable to our NATO maneuvers in Europe."

Meanwhile, the powder keg in Vietnam finally exploded. In the wake of Diem's assassination, Saigon went through a series of violent coups d'état staged by South Vietnamese generals who took turns being "strongman of the month." At the same time, the Viet Cong continued to grow in the Mekong Delta and began exerting their influence in the Central Highlands and the Coastal Plains. In the middle of it all, South Vietnam's army (Army of the Republic of Vietnam—ARVN)[3] remained poorly-led and largely unmotivated.

In August 1964, Congress passed the infamous Gulf of Tonkin Resolution. The new measure was drafted in response to a naval

---

3 Pronounced "arvin."

skirmish involving North Vietnamese boats and the US destroyers *Maddox* and *C. Turner Joy*. Essentially, it gave President Lyndon Johnson the unprecedented authority to use conventional military force in Vietnam without a formal declaration of war. Still, Johnson was confident that he could find a diplomatic solution to the Vietnamese problem.

All that changed, however, on the night of February 15, 1965, when Viet Cong sappers attacked the US airbase at Pleiku. That night, a fed-up Johnson went to his National Security Council and said, "I've had enough of this." The following month, he authorized a systematic bombing campaign and, on March 8, 1965, the first US Marines waded ashore at Danang. Meanwhile, General Westmoreland continued pressing Johnson for more troops. By Westmoreland's estimate, he would need nearly 180,000 troops by the end of 1965.

Among the earliest combat units to arrive with the Class of 1965 was none other than the 1st Cavalry Division (Airmobile), bringing the air cavalry concept into its first wartime proving ground. Still commanded by General Harry WO Kinnard, the Airmobile Division began their operations in the Central Highlands of Vietnam. "Airmobile made history," said Jay. "And from that history, I think we probably revolutionized warfare as much as the domestication of the horse."

At the same time, back in the States, Jay Vanderpool began to feel the squeeze of the growing mission in Vietnam. "We had plenty of money for training before the expanding Vietnam War changed national priorities," he recalled. "Many US Army and US Air Force officers, including general officers, received some excellent training experience [during the annual multi-state maneuvers]."

But before Vietnam could siphon money from Strike Command's training budget, Vanderpool noted that the stateside unit commanders "learned a lot about the capabilities and limitations of tactical units, plus good training in communications and logistics in joint operations." Vanderpool further noted that single-service training exercises tended to operate on a lot of assumptions in maneuvers. "Joint operations force commanders," he said, "tend to use more facts and less theory, just as combined NATO exercises permit realistic appraisals of Allied forces capabilities and limitations." The diversity in terrain also provided a great training opportunity. "An exercise in the rolling, wooded hills of Arkansas and Missouri presents one kind of problem," said Jay. "An exercise across the Colorado River in southern California and Arizona presents entirely different challenges."

Apart from the cyclic training maneuvers, Jay also admired the Strike Command's Military Assistance Program. As the name implied, US military personnel would render assistance and advisory missions to foreign militaries—fostering good ties and foiling potential Communist subversions. One of Strike Command's areas of responsibility was Central Africa. The entire region, most of which was trying to shake off decades of European colonialism, had emerged as a new front (albeit a subdued one) in the ongoing Cold War. Their new domestic governments were a mixed bag of ailing republics and de facto dictatorships. "Some of those governments were really good, or really trying to be," said Jay. "Some were *not* very good; and some weren't trying to be good. It varied a lot."

Logistically, however, each of the Central African armies were a nightmare—"including the Congo," he emphasized.

At the time, Mobutu Sese Seko was Chief of Staff of the Congolese Army. "While I was there," said Vanderpool, "he lined up all the village chiefs politically and, as he already had the Army, it was pretty obvious who was going to be the next president." Mobutu went on to serve as the President of the Democratic Republic of the Congo from 1965 (during its transition into becoming the state of Zaire) until 1997. He soon established the *Popular Movement of the Revolution* as the country's sole political party, and ruled as a dictator until his deposition. Following his exile, Zaire reverted to its former name: Democratic Republic of the Congo.

"It was an interesting experience," he said, particularly when observing the Congolese training centers. "There was a training camp in the Congo on the beach at Banana. The Congolese were given basic rifle training," at the company and battalion level. The Congolese concept of a battalion, however, "looked more like a reinforced company to me," said Jay.

Following their initial training, the Congolese troops would enter parachute training, taught by Israeli commandos. When the Congolese troops got ready to jump, "they had Italian airplanes, Italian pilots, and Israeli jumpmasters," he recalled. "How these recruits out of the bush under stood what was going on, I don't know, because *I* had a hard time following it." Jay sardonically conceded that General Joseph Swing's famous quip about parachute jumping was correct: "The sergeant kicks you out and the ground stops you."

At the same time, Jay was fascinated by how Congolese tribal customs could influence a soldier's perceptions. For instance, one tribal elder (whom Vanderpool referred to as a "witch doctor") had warned his tribesmen against using American rifles. This elder tribesman had said that if a Congolese soldier fired the rifle, its bullets would magically reverse course and hit the soldier right between the eyes."He may have been a pacifist or something," said Jay of the elder.

"Anyway, the troops were afraid to fire their rifles. With some bribery money, clothing and gifts, we hired another 'wise man.' He came up with another theory [to leverage the troops' compliance and allay their fears]." As such, the hired shaman told his Congolese brethren that the bullets would not bounce back to kill them so long as they attached narrow strips of monkey skin to the stocks of their rifles."

Outlandish as it may have seemed, the shaman's advice worked. The Congolese soldiers did as they were told.

"The Israeli parachute commander briefed me on this," said Vanderpool. "I asked if the troops were now firing."

"Yes," the Israeli officer replied. "We're going to fire this afternoon."

Vanderpool, with his curiosity piqued, went down to the range. And, just as the Israeli para-commander had said, every Congolese soldier reported to the range with strips of monkey fur attached to his rifle. Each soldier fired on the range, "and not one man was hit by his own errant bullet, not even a flesh wound," said Jay. "It proves that you learn something wherever you go."

But while Jay Vanderpool was conducting advisory visits and coordinating joint operations within Strike Command, his air cavalry concept had been put to the ultimate test in the highlands of Vietnam. On November 14, 1965, the airmobile troops of 1st Battalion, 7th Cavalry squared off against two regiments of the North Vietnamese Army (NVA) at the Battle of Ia Drang.

Although outnumbered nearly 3-to-1, the Americans won a decisive victory, claiming more than 1,200 enemy soldiers before the NVA quit the field. It was the first major battle between the US Army and North Vietnamese regulars. Although the Americans had won this opening battle, Ia Drang was a critical data point for both sides of the conflict. The opposing forces now had a clear picture of the other's tactics and fighting techniques.

Meanwhile, in Hanoi and in Washington, political and military leaders pondered the implications of this explosive conflict in the Central Highlands of Vietnam. President Johnson was already determined to fight this war on the cheap—not wanting to detract from his "Great Society" programs and other domestic initiatives. He therefore rejected a mass mobilization of the Reserves and National Guard; and he refused to declare a state of emergency, which would have extended the enlistments of the most experienced troops.

Although the Secretary of Defense Robert McNamara had projected a tremendous cost in human lives and resources, his calculations were set aside. Indeed, because American blood had been spilled in such a high-intensity battle, this was America's war now.

Back in Hanoi, however, the NVA had a much brighter outlook. They determined that they had learned enough from the Battle of Ia Drang to defeat (or at least neutralize) the Americans' helicopter advantage. The NVA had been devastated in the Ia Drang campaign, suffering a 12:1 kill-loss ratio in favor of the Americans.

But these body counts were of little concern to Hanoi.

Instead, they focused on something entirely different: The NVA had withstood the awesome firepower of America's military, and felt that they had fought the Americans to a draw. By that metric, they considered such a draw to be the equivalent of a victory. In time, the Communists were certain that they could wear down the Americans just as they had done to the French.

Unfortunately, they were right.

Shortly after the Ia Drang battle, McNamara received a postmission brief in An Khe from Lieutenant Colonel Hal Moore, who had commanded 1st Battalion, 7th Cavalry Regiment during the fight. Moore bluntly described the harsh realities of the Ia Drang campaign. The NVA were no joke: they were well-trained, well-disciplined, and possessed a sort of "suicidal fanaticism," attacking the American lines with unflinching aggression.

As Moore continued that briefing, however, McNamara sat in furrowed silence—suspecting that the war would be difficult to win. On his way back to Washington, McNamara drafted a memo to President Johnson. Within its pages, McNamara outlined two options: go for a diplomatic solution, or rapidly increase the number of US forces in Vietnam. Accordingly, the US would have to send upwards of 600,000 troops if they expected to win. Still, McNamara warned that these deployments would not guarantee success, especially if Red China or the Soviet Union intervened. Plus, US casualties could reach as high as 1,000 per month by 1967.

Nevertheless, Johnson and his advisors decided it was too late to turn back now. If the current kill-loss ratio stayed in favor of the Americans, the White House was certain they could bleed out the enemy within the next few years.

The airmobile commanders, however, were less optimistic.

General Kinnard and his men had already endured one crisis of confidence in the Johnson-McNamara way of war—especially when the President refused to extend enlistments and shipped US forces off to war terribly understrength. Now, in the wake of Ia Drang, men like Harry Kinnard were growing less confident in their leaders' ability to prosecute the war.

As the Airmobile Division endured its trials by fire, however, Vanderpool received an unexpected call from General Jack Norton, the Deputy Commander of United States Army Vietnam. Like

Vanderpool, Norton had been an early pioneer of airmobile warfare during the bureaucratic doldrums of the 1950s. "He wanted to know if I come to Vietnam [from Strike Command] and help on the logistics system behind the Air Cavalry Division."

Jay's reply was simple: "Sure, I'll go if you can get me released here."

It took a near-Herculean effort to release Vanderpool from Strike Command and identify a replacement for the J-4 position, but he finally arrived in Vietnam in the spring of 1966. "I went to Saigon and was assigned to Qui Nhon, which is up the coast north of Saigon. The 1st Cavalry was inland, based at An Khe at that time."

Almost immediately, Jay could tell that Vietnam was a different kind of war. Apart from the local ARVN forces, several Allied partners had joined the effort to roll back the tide of Communism in Southeast Asia. Among the more notable Allied partners were the Australians and the South Koreans. "The Korean Tiger Division [Republic of Korea]," said Jay, "was our local security for Qui Nhon." As the security element, Jay noticed that the Koreans did their own "close-in patrolling"—searching for any signs of VC activity within a prescribed limit of the Qui Nhon base camp. "Combat missions farther out," he said—including the high-profile Search-and-Destroy missions and ambush patrols—"were all handled by the 1st Cavalry Division."

Jay also noticed that the logistics picture was different from what he had seen elsewhere. "I got there right before the big buildup of supplies," he recalled, "and we just started to get our people in." Indeed, this was 1966; the war was young, and public opinion was still generally in favor of the mission.

The logistical anomaly, however, was that the influx of personnel preceded their supplies. "Usually, your supplies get in about a week ahead of your people," said Jay. "I realized . . . that the Airmobile Division was not logistically independent from long lines of communications, and that was one of the reasons I was ordered to Vietnam. I understood airmobile operations and had had some recent experience in logistics. I could make sure that the 1st Cavalry and other airmobile people were supported with their bullets, petrol, and beans."

Thus, to streamline the flow of logistics, and their communication nodes: "I developed what we called logistics task forces," he said. "The concept was simple enough." Every support base would host a logistics task force commander, who would coordinate all levels of logistics to whichever unit they were designated to support. "At An Khe, we had a permanent composite logistics battalion," Jay continued. "As brigade-size combat forces were deployed, we provided a composite logistics task force tailored to support the strengths, weapons, and aircraft of the combat units." These composite task forces were collocated with the combat brigade headquarters.

Thus: "Support was direct. Communications were direct."

Indeed, the command relationship between a tactical unit and their logistics task force was similar to that of an artillery battalion providing fire support to an infantry regiment. Each unit could also provide overlapping tactical security for the other.

As part of their cyclic resupply operations, Vanderpool's task forces provided ammunition, petrol, lubricants, food rations, and various maintenance assets—"but the medical supplies [along with aviation supplies] were on a separate channel of requisition and supply." The logistical apparatus worked well, but Jay often had to contend with commanders and staffs who didn't understand the limits of the Army's supply system.

"They frequently wanted too many supplies," he recalled.

As a logistics commander, he wanted to keep a supply reserve. "Of course, every commander likes to have a reserve." After all, keeping reserves (tactical or logistical) was a well-established part of military science. But, given the maneuver-based culture of the US Army, logistical reserves often became the target of scorn. "If a tactical commander doesn't have a reserve, he's condemned," said Jay. Tactical reserves could save a unit from the jaws of defeat. "If a logistics commander keeps a reserve, he's criticized for being wasteful"—and criticized for hoarding supplies.

But given the fluidity of operational needs, keeping a sizeable logistics reserve would ensure adequate resupply of units in continuous heavy contact. Another liability was that if the logistical reserve got *too* big, they would have to leave behind various supplies when the supporting unit moved to another location.

"This is a constant battle of judgment," said Vanderpool.

He recalled a few instances wherein he was forced to leave a few palettes of ammunition on the ground when the units he supported had to jump to a cross-country location. "We did leave ammunition on the ground sometimes," he admitted, "but for some reason or another it didn't seem to attract the Viet Cong or the North Vietnamese; they left it alone." Likely, the NVA and Viet Cong had little use for ammunition that didn't match the caliber of their own weapons. "We'd go back a week or month later," he said, "with a convoy of maybe some armored personnel carriers and some gunships to bring it [the ammunition] out." And every time Vanderpool's men returned to their abandoned palettes, the ammunition would be untouched by the enemy.

Still, the logistics task forces worked out very well for ensuring delivery of supply. "But we didn't always have tactical commanders who were too enthusiastic," he admitted. "Some were so solicitous, we could hardly do our job. They were worried about our safety"—or so they claimed. Still, with every resupply or recovery mission, Vanderpool's logistics teams went in riding shotgun aboard Huey gunships, or had some kind of heavily-armed escort. In fact, he recalled that: "We had very, very little trouble," from the NVA or Viet Cong. Beyond a few land mines or stationary explosives, neither Vanderpool nor any of his support troops received much harassment from the enemy. "We never got into anything like the French go into in the pass between An Khe and Pleiku," he said, "where a lot of people got hurt"—referring to the massacre of the French *Groupement Mobile 100* in 1954.

Reflecting on his time as a logistics commander in Vietnam, Jay likened his task forces to the Mobile Army General Supply Point he had seen in Europe. "That was the same general concept," he said, "on a different scale and for a different customer." It became a case study in how to provide long-term logistics to light infantry forces on an expeditionary role. "I had worked with the Marines earlier in my life [Guadalcanal and in the Pacific campaigns] and they'd always had this problem . . . they can't sustain heavy combat operations for long periods, very far from the beachhead [or landing zone]."

To affect the timely logistical support of units in the field, Vanderpool ultimately built logistics bases at An Khe, Pleiku, Kontum and other areas where the brigades might be fighting on any given month. "I was alternately commander or deputy commander of the Qui Nhon support command," he recalled. "We supported combat operations westward to Cambodia and Laos. We built up Qui Nhon to a pretty good wartime logistics base."

Indeed, it became a workable hub, even if the harbor wasn't ideal.

"We installed a Delong pier to handle four ships. Much of our cargo came ashore in landing craft. We were receiving 12,000 tons a day when I left." Although Jay was encouraged by the volume of equipment arriving into theater, it was more than his supply depots could feasibly handle. Almost daily, the Qui Nhon logistics center was receiving more supplies than they had warehousing to hold it.

To make matters worse, Jay's supply centers were understaffed.

"We were chronically short of qualified logistics people. We normally had 30 or more cargo ships tied up offshore. Our transportation system was more efficient than our receiving and storage system." The need to declutter his logistical centers meant that Vanderpool had to personally deliver supplies to a brigade in enemy contact (i.e. actively engaging the Viet Cong in battle) three or four times a week. As such, he knew each of the brigade commanders quite well. "Our logistics system of course was simpler for the ground-based people than it was for the airmobile people, because they didn't jump around so much."

In May 1966, General Jack Norton assumed command of the 1st Cavalry Division when General Kinnard redeployed to the US. Almost simultaneously, Vanderpool noticed an uptick in the volume and frequency of incoming troop waves. "We had brigades coming and going around there from the 101st Airborne and other outfits," he said. "We also got the 4th Infantry Division."

By the summer of 1966, Allied progress against the Viet Cong and NVA had been slow, but encouraging. By the standards of attrition warfare, the Americans were well ahead in the game. Despite heavy losses, they had won a hard-earned victory at Ia Drang and throughout the Central Highlands in 1965. Now, during the first half of the New Year, MACV had cast its eyes toward the enemy stronghold in the coastal province of Binh Dinh. The goal had been to break the Viet Cong's grip over the eastern parts of the province, whose agricultural produce was vital to South Vietnam.

American tactical forces succeeded in clearing the VC from Binh Dinh and the surrounding area, but it was soon clear that MACV had no plan to coordinate South Vietnamese government operations to reestablish control in the areas where the enemy had been cleared. This allowed the Viet Cong and NVA to retake large swaths of land from which they had previously been ousted. Thus, it raised the question: If MACV and Saigon couldn't keep the VC/NVA cabal from returning to Binh Dinh—where the most powerful American forces had crushed enemy forces—how could they re-establish South Vietnamese control in other regions where the US military presence wasn't as strong? But the war was young, and the American public still strongly supported it. In the meantime, men like Jay Vanderpool could do little more than hope that the military would achieve its objectives in Vietnam.

Those objectives, however, were unclear even to America's leadership. And the perennially poor decisions coming out of the Johnson White House only compounded the problem. In 1966, for example, Johnson announced that the standard tour of duty for all troops in Vietnam would be twelve months (except the Marines who were given thirteen month rotations). Under this policy, the GIs who had gained the most critical knowledge of how to survive in Vietnam would be going home, taking all their experience and expertise with them. Replacing them would be an ever-growing force of draftees, replaced in turn by newer draftees, whose quality of training would fall ever lower as the demand for manpower grew.

For Jay Vanderpool, however, his yearlong tour in Southeast Asia was coming to an end, and he was eager to get home. "I caught a plane out of Pleiku, landed in San Francisco and flew home." For his service in Vietnam, he was awarded his fifth Legion of Merit.

"I was assigned to Headquarters, Third Army at Fort McPherson, Georgia. As the Deputy G-4, Deputy Logistics chief. This didn't particularly appeal to me as it was mostly posts, camps, commissaries and peacetime rationing and budgeting."

More to the point, he was getting bored of Army life.

"I had already completed a little over 30 years of service," he said, "and I was very tired." Indeed, for much of the past decade, he had been working a perennial seven-day work week. After serving in three of America's greatest conflicts—World War II, Korea, and now Vietnam—"I was mentally and physically tired . . . burned out."

After some brief introspection, he said out loud: "Oh, the heck with it. I think I'll just quit." Jay Dee Vanderpool retired at the rank of Colonel in March 1967, culminating more than 30 years of active service.

Not wanting to venture too far from the American Southeast, he and his wife Lynn settled in Sarasota, Florida, where they spent the remainder of their lives as a retired couple. Having spent a number of years in the Tampa Bay area during Jay's tour at MacDill Air Force Base, the couple had grown quite fond of the Florida Gulf Coast.

In his later years, Vanderpool referred to Sarasota as a "nice little town on the west coast of Florida: A cultural center, good fishing, boating, libraries, theaters, and performing arts. In fact, it's just about the cultural center of Florida. If it isn't in Miami, it's probably here."

Having spent thirty years of his life at the forefront of America's biggest wars, he was happy to live a quiet life in retirement. But his legacy in the United States Army would live on for generations. For on June 4, 1977, Jay Vanderpool was inducted into the Army Aviation Association of America's Hall of Fame at Fort Rucker, Alabama. His award citation reads:

In 1956, he began experimentation on ordnance and airmobile tactics for Army helicopters. Colonel Vanderpool overcame a multitude of barriers through aggressive dedication to duty and superior leadership. He and his team developed, tested, and proved the feasibility, practicality, and potential tactical effectiveness of the armed helicopter, which abetted their air assault tactics that led to the armed helicopter's later combat success.

Colonel Vanderpool sold this new concept to both military and civilian leaders through his team's presentation of live fire demonstrations. Through these demonstrations, the groundwork was laid for the air assault concept which was later employed by the 11th Air Assault Division whose tactics we still draw upon today. Army Aviation's lineage from Colonel Vanderpool is very much alive. It links us closely to facts about helicopter hardware, armament, tactics, and, perhaps most important, the esprit de corps and the vision that Colonel Vanderpool created.

Jay Vanderpool then returned to his quiet life in Sarasota, where he lived until his passing on July 16, 1993. He was 76 years old.

Epilogue

Understanding Vanderpool's Legacy

Jay D. Vanderpool was a man of true pioneer stock. His was the roughand-rural upbringing reminiscent of Daniel Boone, Jim Bridger, and Jedidiah Smith. Early in his life, he acquired the skills of a hunter, trapper, and outdoorsmen to a level that most Americans (even in the early 20th Century) could never match. Although the details of his young family life remain vague—coming mostly from genealogical records—one can surmise that Jay Vanderpool did not necessarily have a happy childhood.

Considering that Bessie and Dixon Vanderpool's marriage ended in divorce, one can safely assume that their union was not a happy one. By Jay's own admission, he never saw his father again after the divorce. However, his father didn't pass away until 1941, more than a decade after the marriage ended. Thus, it raises the question: Why did the family patriarch never re-establish contact with any of his sons?

Did the mother engage in parental alienation?
Did the father willfully abandon the family?
Whatever the case, neither Jay nor his brothers made any attempt to find Dixon after their mother's death. This family dynamic might explain why Jay spent most of his time outdoors—camping,

hunting, trapping, and fishing. Perhaps it was his means of escapism from an unhappy life at home.

Of particular interest is that Jay Vanderpool seemed to enjoy his time in the CCC (and his time as a young itinerant worker) *more* than his childhood in the American Southwest. But his early forays into the great outdoors, the Civilian Conservation Corps, and the transient lifestyle gave him a sense of rugged individualism and self--reliance that matured him far beyond most of his contemporaries. These metaphysical skills undoubtedly gave him an advantage when he joined the US Army during the throes of the Great Depression in 1936. He had no aspirations to be a career soldier, much less a career officer; but he found that he took well to the military lifestyle.

Some say that "success" happens when hard work and talent meet opportunity. Such was the case when Jay Vanderpool landed in Hawaii. Through his hard work and dedication, he distinguished himself as an exemplary NCO; and despite being a high school dropout, he was selected for Officer Candidate School. Although fate cast a grim shadow upon Pearl Harbor in December 1941, Jay would again distinguish himself on the frontlines in the burgeoning war against the Empire of Japan.

Surviving the Battles of Guadalcanal and New Georgia, Jay Vanderpool leveraged his hard-nosed patrolling and tracking skills to become an impromptu "commando," infiltrating the Philippine Islands via submarine to coordinate operations between the indigenous guerrillas and Allied conventional forces. He was, effectively, at the forefront of the newly-emerging field of Special Operations. Having honed his skills as a "tactical liaison" behind enemy lines in World War II, he put those skills to use again on the battlefields of North Korea. Mobilizing partisan forces against the North Koreans and Red Chinese, he provided a lasting case study on how to leverage unconventional forces to facilitate strategic victories.

But perhaps his most enduring legacy lies in the realm of airmobile warfare. During the 1950s, when most of the Pentagon had little interest (and even less regard) for helicopters, Jay Vanderpool swam against the tide of bureaucratic resentment, creating an armed rotary-winged platform and with a foundational set of tactical doctrines. From these developments came the broader and more--detailed constructs of helicopter warfare that we know today. Vanderpool's diligence (and the diligence of several others) in shaping the concepts of air cavalry laid the foundations for the success of American airmobile units in Vietnam.

Today, Jay D. Vanderpool's legacy endures as a man of remarkable resilience, ruggedness, and determination. He embodied the collective spirit of the Greatest Generation; a man who emerged from the throes of the Dust Bowl and became a key player in the realm of unconventional warfare, as well as a "founding father" of the US Army's air cavalry.

Select Bibliography

Primary Sources

Flanagan, Edward M. *The Angels: A History of the 11th Airborne.* Random House: New York, 1990.

Moore, Hal, and Joseph Galloway. *We Were Soldiers Once...and Young.* Random House: New York, 1992.

The Jay D. Vanderpool Papers, 1953–1983. A collection of Jay Vanderpool's various papers, correspondence, unit histories, and an oral history covering his life and military career. Eight (8) boxes. US Army Military History Institute: Carlisle Barracks, 1983.

The Jay D. Vanderpool Photograph Collection, 1955–1977. A collection of more than 170 photographs covering Jay Vanderpool's service from his time at Fort Rucker through his service in Vietnam. One (1) box. US Army Military History Institute: Carlisle Barracks, 1983.

Vanderpool, Jay D. "We Armed the Helicopters." *US Army Aviation Digest*, June 1971.

Walthall, Melvin C. *Lightning Forward: A History of the 25th Infantry Division (Tropic Lightning) 1941–1978.* The 25th Infantry Division Assoc: Honolulu, 1979.

Secondary Sources

Carland, John. *Combat Operations: Stemming the Tide, May 1965-October 1966*. (US Army in Vietnam Series). US Army Center for Military History: Washington DC, 2000.

Fehrenbach, TR. *This Kind of War*. Potomac Books: Sterling, 1995.

Johnson, Lawrence H. *Winged Sabers: The Air Cavalry in Vietnam*. Stackpole Books: Mechanicsville, 1990.

Krivdo, Michael. "Major Jay D. Vanderpool: Advisor to the Philippine Guerrillas." *Veritas*, vol.9, no.1, 2013.

Krivdo, Michael. "Creating an Army Guerrilla Command—Part 1: The First Six Months." *Veritas*, vol. 8, no. 2, 2012.

Krivdo, Michael. "The Army's Guerrilla Command in Korea—Part II: The Rest of the Story." *Veritas*, vol. 9, no. 1, 2012.

Tolson, John J. *Airmobility in Vietnam*. (Vietnam Studies Series). US Army Center for Military History: Washington DC, 1981.

Notes

1 Equivalent to $17.07 per hour in 2022 dollars.
2 "Dunkirk" refers to the wholesale evacuation of British troops from the shores of northern France in 1940. British forces retreated from mainland Europe before regrouping and coming back strong during the Battle of Britain.
3 This reorganization was part of the US Army's transition to the "triangular" division concept. Under the terms of this reorganization, the 8th Artillery Regiment was officially re-designated as a "battalion" in 1941. However, for the purposes of this chapter, I often refer to the unit as a "regiment" in the colloquial sense, even though it ceased to carry this designation by December 1941.
4 Vanderpool never provides an exact date for this alleged briefing. Moreover, he stated that he only "believes" it was General Walter Short who gave the brief. It is plausible, however, that General Short would have been the one to deliver to these remarks, as he was the commander of US Army forces in Hawaii. Did such a meeting between FDR and General Short take place? Was there truly an official estimate of January 1? Those answers lie beyond the scope of this book. Jay Vanderpool, however, confirms that this was the information he received in the briefing.
5 So-named for the Gifu Prefecture on the main island of Honshu in Japan.

6 Following World War II, Davis remained in the Army and later served in Korea and Vietnam. He retired in 1972 at the rank of Colonel. He passed away in 1991.
7 In modern parlance, these operations are known as "danger close" fire missions, bringing artillery support to friendly troops in closer-quarters combat while mitigating the risks of fratricide.
8 The attack on the Philippine Islands occurred almost simultaneously with the attack on Pearl Harbor. Because of the International Date Line, however, the concurrent date in the Philippines was December 8.
9 Like Vanderpool, many of Dick Ferriter's missions would take him behind enemy lines. Ferriter retired from the Army in 1972 at the rank of colonel. His son, Mike Ferriter, is a retired 3-star general and a veteran of the wars in Iraq and Somalia.
10 Whitney would later preside over the US military government in Occupied Japan.
11 Simultaneously, the Far East Command retained its own, organic special operations unit.
12 A 1942 West Point graduate, Koster later gained notoriety as the commander of the 23d Infantry (Americal) Division during the My Lai Massacre in Vietnam.
13 Later, UNPFK operations expanded to include the east coast of the Korean Peninsula as well.
14 Vanderpool did not specify who these sewing girls were, but they may have been South Korean contract seamstresses.
15 Throughout these partisan campaigns, Jay Vanderpool spent most of his time at the regimental and/or battalion level. "Below that level, no one spoke English," he said. And the American advisors at the company level and below had to rely on interpreters. "I preferred to operate from regimental

headquarters, and only with battalions during critical periods," he continued. "Regiments normally controlled three or four islands. The regimental commanders coordinated the defense of those several islands. From their headquarters, you could learn more than you could on an island with one battalion, unless there was something critical going on there." Vanderpool's main base was in Seoul and, as he recalled: "I spent most of my time there for communication reasons."

16 Jean Bastien-Thiry would later attempt to assassinate President Charles De Gaulle in 1962. The failed assassination attempt made international headlines and inspired Frederick Forsyth's novel, *The Day of the Jackal*, published in 1971.

About the Author
Mike Guardia

Mike Guardia is an internationally-recognized author and military historian. A veteran of the United States Army, he served six years on active duty as an Armor Officer. He is the author of the widely-acclaimed *Hal Moore: A Soldier Once . . . and Always*, the first-ever biography chronicling the life of LTG Harold G. Moore, whose battlefield leadership was popularized by the film *We Were Soldiers*, starring Mel Gibson.

He was named "Author of the Year" in 2021 by the Military Writers Society of America, and has been nominated twice for the Army Historical Foundation's Distinguished Book Award.

As a speaker, he has given presentations at the US Special Operations Command, the George HW Bush Presidential Library, the First Division Museum, and the US 7th Infantry Division Headquarters at Fort Lewis.

In 2022, he appeared in the History Channel series, *I Was There*, cast as a featured historian in the episodes on the Johnstown Flood of 1889, the Chernobyl Disaster, the Battle of Stalingrad, and the Oklahoma City Bombing. His other media appearances include guest spots on *National Public Radio* (NPR); *Frontlines of Freedom*; *Armada International*; and *Military Network Radio*.

His work has been reviewed in the *Washington Times*, *Military Review*, *Vietnam Magazine*, *DefenceWeb South Africa*, and *Soldier Magazine UK*. He holds a BA and MA in American History from the University of Houston; and an MA in Education from the University of St. Thomas. He currently lives in Minnesota.

www.ingramcontent.com/pod-product-compliance
Lightning Source LLC
LaVergne TN
LVHW051829080426
835512LV00018B/2791